TO:
Kurt + Nancy)

For Toms 75th

Live to Eat!
Enjoy the book.

NICHOLAS

Published by Pediment Publishing, a division of The Pediment Group, Inc. www.pediment.com Printed in Canada

NICHOLAS

By Nicholas Harary

with Peter Zuorick

Edited by Joseph D'Angelo

Photography by Steve Legato

Designed by Chris Fenison, Pediment Publishing

Dedicated to Melissa, Nicholas and Juliana.
Melissa, you are my inspiration and the love of my life.
Nicholas and Juliana, seeing the smiles on your faces and
looking at life through your eyes makes it all worth it.

Acknowledgments

The *Restaurant Nicholas Cookbook* is a collaborative effort and would not exist without some key individuals. First and foremost, I would like to thank my loyal customers for their unwavering dedication over the last nine years. Your continued support and encouragement helped my little restaurant in the suburbs become a success.

I would like to thank the entire staff of Restaurant Nicholas. Without their hard work and dedication there would be no restaurant, let alone a cookbook. Special thanks to the kitchen staff, especially my two chef de cuisines, Manuel Perez and David Santos. Both led pivotal roles in the development of these recipes.

I would also like to thank Peter Zuorick and Joseph D'Angelo for their contributions to the writing and editing of this project. Were it not for their tireless work, this cookbook would just be a collection of misspelled and grammatically incorrect recipes.

I am forever grateful for the beautiful photos taken by Steve Legato, one of the world's best food photographers. The shear brilliance of his photos speaks for itself.

Thanks to all the guys back in my pizza days. Many of the valuable lessons I learned working with them still apply to my daily regimen.

Thanks to George Hauer for taking the time to teach me the nuts and bolts of how a successful restaurant is run.

Special thanks to James Maggs, my attorney, consultant and friend. I don't know how we would have opened Restaurant Nicholas without his legal advice and support.

I would like to thank my mother, from whom I inherited an incredible work ethic. How she raised two kids with hardly any money will always inspire me.

Special thanks to Ron Szczepanski, my stepfather, for helping my mother through the darkest days.

Most importantly, I would like to thank my wife, Melissa. Restaurant Nicholas would be nothing without her. She is my muse. The cuisine of the restaurant is as elegant as it is because I am always trying to impress her. I don't know if I would have opened a place like Restaurant Nicholas were it not for her. She is my inspiration.

Table of Contents

The Restaurant Nicholas Story

NICHOLAS IS BORN

On the morning of April 12, 2007, I am not thinking about the restaurant. For the first time in six years my focus is elsewhere—specifically the maternity ward of Riverview Hospital, where my wife, Melissa, just gave birth to my son. Baby Nicholas and his beautiful mother are doing just fine. Our parents are present, mothers crying (naturally). I am bursting with joy as I hold my son, still wrapped in his baby blue delivery blanket. At this moment, Restaurant Nicholas is the furthest thing from my mind.

But the tranquility doesn't last long.

The cellphone in my pocket buzzes incessantly. I try to ignore it. Looking at my son, I can already tell he is NFL worthy. Maybe it's the New York Giants, I think in an attempt to stave off the inevitable with a bit of humor. Maybe they heard the news and are already trying to claim this future all-pro. His arm looks strong. Or maybe it's the Yankees looking to sign their next ace pitcher.

Unfortunately, it isn't any pro team. It isn't even friends or family calling with congratulations. Sadly, it's David Santos, my chef de cuisine.

"Nicholas, there's five inches of water on the kitchen floor!" he says. "Water is everywhere. It's coming up through the drains."

I instantly snap out of my new-father euphoria. When we redesigned the restaurant a few years ago, the kitchen was built below the water table. Four pumps were installed to safeguard against flooding, but if they malfunctioned for some reason, the consequences would be disastrous. Worst case scenario: the foundation is permanently damaged and the building would have to come down. My lifelong dream of owning a fine-dining restaurant reduced to a pile of rubble.

"I'll be right there, Dave. By the way, I'm a dad."

"That's great, congratulations! Just hurry up, please. The water is starting to smell."

My son is barely 15 minutes old and here I am darting back to the restaurant. If you think being a restaurateur is as glamorous as it appears on the Food Network, you're severely delusional. Sometimes it seems like it's one catastrophe after the next. While the kitchen flood on the day of my son's birth was a terrible crisis, it doesn't even rank among the worst we've been through.

As a restaurateur, you need to be resilient. You're on the clock 24/7 whether it's your day off or, in this case, the birth of your first child. Welcome to my world. Pretty glamorous, huh?

People wrongly assume that Restaurant Nicholas was financed by my wealthy parents. Or that I led a privileged childhood and was afforded the luxury to apprentice under the best European chefs. Sorry to disappoint, but nothing could be further from the truth. I grew up in the Bronx, and my family life was less than perfect. I worked in a pizzeria when I was 11. While the neighborhood kids were outside riding their bikes, I was busting my hump in a kitchen. I may not have known it at the time, but the combination of long hours and hot ovens would be the foundation of my future.

From a very young age, I believed that hard work pays off in the end. As I grew older, I never let go of this concept. I tried to be the best I could be and absorb as much information as I could along the way. From culinary school to my time in California and New York to opening Restaurant Nicholas in 2000, I always adhered to those principles.

The story of Restaurant Nicholas is the classic underdog tale. It was built on the hard work and determination of myself, Melissa and, of course, my tireless staff. We are not the best restaurant in the world. I am not the best chef in the world, nor am I the best businessman. However, what you see and what you eat and drink at the restaurant is the best that we can give you.

I hope this book will be inspirational to you. Not to open a restaurant necessarily, but to be the best at whatever it is you do.

THE EARLY YEARS

My life didn't always revolve around four-star cuisine. My childhood was all but void of culinary epiphanies. When I was first exposed to the restaurant business, I wanted to be a pizza man. Strangely, it was a troubled family life that led me down this path.

My father was abusive, and I remember some terrible episodes because of him. Eventually, my mother took my sister and me and left him. As the divorce was being processed, we moved nearly every six months just so my father couldn't find us. My mother worked in northern New Jersey, so we were limited to living in New Jersey and New York City.

We were constantly living in fear, always having to look over our shoulders to make sure my father wasn't around. As hard as we tried though, he always seemed to find us. This usually led to serious conflict and violence. As a child, it was a scary and confusing time.

One unforgettable incident resulted in my mother being hospitalized. Instead of trying to help, I hid in the closet beneath a pile of laundry, paralyzed with fear. I felt like a coward. Even though I now realize there wasn't much a 9-year-old boy could have done, that feeling of helplessness tore me to pieces inside. My mother and sister were the only two people in my life and I let them both down.

From that day on, I swore that I would never let myself be scared of anyone ever again. I would never let a situation spin out of my control. A fire was lit inside me that would define me as the person I am today.

Shortly after the divorce became official, my father ended up in jail. My mother did her best to support us, but after the court fees and hospital bills, we were on a very tight budget. Luxuries like cable TV and air conditioning were out of the question in our tiny New Jersey apartment. In the summer, I stayed cool by walking around air-conditioned stores. My favorite place to hang out was a small eatery called Pizzarama, right down the street from our home. It was air conditioned and they had a few video games. Being new to the area, I didn't have any friends, so I passed the afternoons in the pizzeria, pumping quarters into those games.

The owner, Mike, seemed to like me. Occasionally, I would pitch in and wipe down some tables in exchange for a slice of pizza and a soda. I started spending more and more time at Pizzarama, and Mike eventually offered me a part-time job bussing tables and sweeping floors. I liked making my own money and not having to rely on my mother. I also fell in love with the camaraderie of the kitchen.

I became part of a team, as dysfunctional as it may have been. Kitchen jargon like "hot," "behind," and "sharp" became second nature to me. We would argue about sports nearly every day, with plenty of gambling to back it up. I apprenticed under some of the world's best ball-breakers, who taught me the skills that I believe I have perfected as an adult. They may not have been the greatest role models for a young boy, but they were my new family and I enjoyed every second I spent at Pizzarama.

Despite the fun I was having with the guys, the job was hard and often thankless. I worked every weekend, day and night. As I got older, I was promoted to dishwasher, then sandwich cook, then finally pizza maker, a very coveted position. By this time, I was working six days and nearly 50 hours a week. I would go to the pizzeria directly from school, work all night, go home, do my homework, and then do it all over again the next day. I was getting good at what I did. Spinning pizzas had become wired into my nervous system. I was fast and knew my way around a pizza oven.

I worked at Pizzarama until I was about 15, then took a job at an Italian restaurant. It was a little more upscale than Pizzarama, offering lasagna and a variety of pasta dishes. The hours were long and the work was hard, but I didn't mind. I had begun to envision myself doing this for the rest of my life. As much as the chef tried desperately to talk me out of it, I had made up my mind. I was going to become a chef.

After graduating from high school in 1991, at the age of 17, I set my sights on culinary school. At the time, culinary schools were only accepting older, more experienced applicants, but the Culinary Institute of America in Hyde Park, New York, was willing to test the waters with students a bit younger. After all, despite my age, I did have six years of experience under my belt. Financing the tuition with the money saved from working all those hours, I enrolled in the CIA that fall.

I was the youngest student in school. The average age of my classmates was 25. Although most had more sophisticated cooking backgrounds than I did, I was not intimidated. My confidence level was through the roof. They may have known more than me, but I knew more than they did when they were my age.

I spent all of my free time studying, which, for a college student, is a lot easier to do when he doesn't drink and is too young to go to bars. I wasn't concerned with what I was going to do after class. Instead, I looked forward to the next time I was *in* class. Besides learning about food and wine,

I was also taught restaurant management—lessons which would prove invaluable down the line.

I graduated the two-year program with honors, never missing a single minute of class. At 19, I was eager to continue learning all I could about the restaurant business. Opening a restaurant of my own was not a dream for me, but a solid goal. Nothing was going to stop me.

Throughout the next few years, I worked several jobs, from bartender to kitchen manager, in a variety of restaurants in order to further my knowledge of the restaurant business. Before long, I knew about mixing drinks, managing people, taking inventory, waiting tables, recommending wine, calming difficult customers, pampering VIPs, hiring, firing, and payroll—in short, every aspect of running a successful restaurant.

During this period, I met Melissa, who was also in the restaurant business. After working throughout New Jersey, we moved to Southern California, where we were exposed to fantastic vineyards and California cuisine. I took a job at George's at the Cove in San Diego, where the owner, George Hauer, would become one of my biggest influences. George took me under his wing and taught me the nuts and bolts of the restaurant business. In exchange for me educating his staff about wine, he helped me create a business plan for my future restaurant.

After two years, we moved back to New York, where Melissa took a job as dining room director at the well-respected Tabla. With my knowledge of wine now fine-tuned from working at George's, I landed a job as head sommelier at the four-star Jean Georges, which was and still is one of the best restaurants in the world. As the only non-European sommelier, customers really seemed to appreciate my down-to-earth approach to wine. During my two years at Jean Georges, I saw that it wasn't magic that made Jean-Georges Vongerichten and his restaurant a success. Rather, a combination of hard work and an educated staff afforded him his four stars.

Once again, it was time to move on. Looking back, New York was sort of a finishing school for Melissa and me, educating us on the little details that can turn an ordinary restaurant into a special one. Before we left New York, Melissa and I were married.

At 25, I certainly didn't know everything there was about the restaurant business, but I knew enough... enough to start turning my longtime goal into a reality.

ELVIS HAS LEFT THE BUILDING

Years of sacrifice and tireless work were about to be put to the test. I was going to open a restaurant and I was going to do it on my terms. I devised a business plan that was foolproof. For starters, I didn't want any investors or partners. My restaurant would be owned and operated solely by Melissa and myself.

The restaurant would also have to be a stand-alone building, nothing in a strip mall. We looked at numerous locations from Connecticut to Southern California, eventually deciding on New Jersey, which I saw as uncharted territory. At the time, the Garden State had a few fine-dining restaurants, but most were old fixtures which hadn't adjusted their menus for nearly a decade. It was time for a change.

The Mexican restaurant Los Amigos was located on a major highway in the Red Bank area. The only building on the site, it was recently put on the market. Most importantly, it had a liquor license—the third condition of my plan.

I set up an appointment with the title holder, whom we'll call "Elvis" because he was an exact replica of the King, from his jet black pompadour and pork-chop sideburns to his blue suede shoes. He even had the Elvis sunglasses. Only he was Greek. He explained to me in his thick accent that he recently sold the property to a Mexican couple, but when they couldn't pay their bills, he stepped back in and resumed ownership.

I thought it strange that someone would sell a property only to buy it back a short time later. Well, Elvis never wholly sold the property to the couple. He surrendered ownership but held a note on the building until he was paid back. When the new owners couldn't stay ahead of the bills, Elvis repossessed the building along with any repairs and renovations that had been made. I found out that this wasn't the only time Elvis had sold and later reclaimed the property. He was running a scam: sell the building and its liquor license at a low price, then when the business failed, take it back, usually in better condition than when he left it. It was quite a lucrative operation, I had to admit. I'm sure when he set his eyes on this 25-year-old kid, he saw dollar signs.

Elvis was asking $650,000 for everything: the building, the land and the liquor license. In New Jersey, a liquor license alone can be priced upwards of $500,000, so I was sitting on a pretty good deal. I just couldn't fall prey to Elvis's scam. Elvis used the low price as bait, assuming no one would be able to do anything with this broken down building. Eventually they would be forced to return it. If I was to beat Elvis at his own game, I had to string him along and never let on that I was planning to buy the building outright.

I went to the Small Business Administration to begin the process of financing the deal. The SBA doesn't grant loans, only guarantees them. I still had to find a bank crazy enough to lend me $650,000. Believe it or not, there was such an institution willing to take a chance on an ambitious kid with aspirations far bigger than his bank account.

After six months of jumping through hoops for Elvis, the SBA and the bank, it was time to close the deal. That morning, Melissa and I were admittedly nervous as we drove to the restaurant. Our 1989 Ford Probe, with its blown clutch, bucked into a parking slot alongside the only other cars in the lot: two Mercedes, a Porsche and Elvis's Cadillac. The driver's side door was completely useless, so I hopped over the center console and we both exited through the passenger side. One of the retractable headlights—the one that worked— remained up as if winking at the other vehicles.

Elvis had no idea there was going to be a bank representative at the meeting, not to mention my lawyer. Assuming that I would pay him off in installments, as every other buyer had done, he was visibly concerned.

He wasn't the only one. At this point, the bank representative had never met me in person. All interaction had been done online or over the phone. Because of my extensive résumé, he must have thought I was at least in my early thirties.

It was quickly apparent that neither the bank nor Elvis wanted to close this deal. Perhaps it was my age. Or maybe it was because the Los Amigos property was in such appalling shape. Over the next nine hours, they looked for every way out. It was too late, though. I had done my homework and my lawyer was better than theirs.

When all the papers were signed, Melissa and I were the only people in the room smiling. I invited everyone to the opening night of the restaurant, but I don't think anyone but

Below: The would-be Restaurant Nicholas, 1950s.

us thought that day would ever come. As we walked back to our car and both slid in through the passenger side door, we were ecstatic. I pulled out of the parking lot and waved to Elvis and the bank rep. Their sour expressions suggested that they were still trying to figure out whether they had been duped. The bum clutch on the old Probe bucked violently as I took off down the highway. The one working headlight shone in the night, as if it were winking.

ONE CRAZY SCHEME

We had our restaurant, but it was no time to celebrate. There was still a great deal of work to be done. Remodeling the old building would cost around $300,000—and that was just for cement and steel. It didn't account for chairs, tables, silverware, new windows or a new carpet. I could barely afford to put gas in the Ford Probe, let alone shell out a chunk of change like this.

I couldn't let the cost stop me after I had already come this far. The show had to go on. As shocking as my accumulated debt looked on paper—somewhere in the $450,000 range—I had presumed this might happen. So a few months earlier, I devised a plan. It was a long shot, but I was going to go for it.

We've all received them in the mail: "You have been pre-approved for a credit card!" You probably just throw them away with the rest of the junk mail. If you applied for every credit card offered, you might have upwards of 30 cards totaling tens of thousands of dollars in credit. Who needs that much credit? At this point, I did.

For a few weeks, I collected all the applications I received, filled them out, and set them aside. When the time was right, I would send them all out simultaneously with the hope that they would be approved at nearly the same time. I would have tens of thousands of dollars in credit, more or less, in one sweeping blow. I thought it was The Great American Scam. Melissa thought differently.

"This is ridiculous, Nicholas. It will never work." She had a valid concern. If my plan failed, not only would we be in life-altering debt, but the embarrassment would force us to move out of the state. Reluctantly, Melissa went along with my crazy scheme and began saving our "junk mail."

Meanwhile, problems with the building began to pile up. Yet every day I would show up to the construction site with the confidence of someone who's done this before. When the builder told me the air conditioners needed to be replaced, I smiled and said, "Okay," as if I already knew this would happen. Despite my optimistic stance, we were getting closer and closer to the financial breaking point.

On a positive note, the restaurant was slowly coming together. It felt good to see the once rundown building blossoming into the restaurant I've always wanted. In the main dining room, the old Sheetrock ceiling was torn down to reveal an open space which made the room look twice as big. I didn't think that was such a bad thing. Unfortunately, the other shoe was about to drop.

The following day, the room was given its standard inspection to see if everything was up to code. There, it was brought to my attention that the ceiling was so vast because all the

support beams had been removed! You could see where they were crudely hacked out. For some reason, the previous owners thought it would be a good idea to remove all of the load-bearing elements from the ceiling. It might have been the worst idea ever. If there was a blizzard or heavy winds, the roof could conceivably collapse. My worst nightmare had become reality: the entire building would have to come down.

As I wondered how I was ever going to pay for this, I remembered all the people throughout this ordeal who told me not to buy this building. For the first time, I wished I had taken their advice.

That night, smiling through clenched teeth, I said to Melissa, "It's that time." We sent out all of the credit card applications and soon had $225,000 in credit. My plan worked with little time to spare.

I spoke to several construction companies to see if there was a way to salvage the dining room without tearing the whole building down. Thankfully, one had the idea to support the roof with tie beams and knock the building out from underneath it. This option was far cheaper than razing the entire building, so we went with it.

We were back on track. With the new line of credit, construction continued. Bills were paid and I even bought new chairs, silverware, windows and carpets. To keep our expenses to a minimum, Melissa and I lived in the basement of our townhouse and rented out the upstairs. As much as we needed a new car—or at least get the one we shared fixed—we commuted to work together each day in the beat-up Ford Probe. We transferred the credit balances back and forth between cards to avoid late fees and take advantage of low interest rates. For Melissa, this had become a full-time job.

With a mountain of credit card debt and no practical experience in getting a business off the ground, Melissa and I were on the verge of opening our restaurant.

OR SO WE THOUGHT

In our early brainstorming sessions, I envisioned a European dining experience similar to what Melissa and I encountered during our travels in France. The dining room décor would be deliberately understated. There would be no music. The restaurant would stand solely on great food and service. Everything else was just fluff. Guests would leisurely enjoy a multi-course meal spanning a few hours. It would be as if you were dining in a small French village like Beaune. After being open for a few days, however, I quickly realized that Beaune is miles away from Middletown, New Jersey.

We quietly opened our doors in November 2000 with just 55 seats in the dining room. Our small staff consisted of Melissa and me, Chef de Cuisine Cory Heyer, three captains, three servers, two cooks and one dishwasher. Our first week's customers seemed happy. No one complained about the food or the service. But my European recreation was not unfolding the way I had hoped. The combination of the minimalist furnishings and lack of music was awkward. The guests felt compelled to whisper as if they were in a library. An average table sat for one and a half hours, about three hours less than I had anticipated. After the guests left, the table was empty for the rest of the evening.

"Oh shit, this isn't going to work," I thought to myself, peering into a half-filled, uncomfortably silent dining room. I had created a VFW hall, albeit a very elegant one. It was bad. Melissa knew it, too. We wouldn't last a year like this. I needed to make some adjustments "on the fly," as we say in the kitchen.

The next morning, I bought a boom box. It would have to do for the time being. I rigged it up at the service bar in the back of the dining room. That night, there was music and an immediate difference in the dining room. The guests were more relaxed. They were no longer whispering. The room felt warmer. A few weeks later, I had a sound system professionally installed.

We still had the dilemma of making the restaurant feel full and lively throughout the night. Originally, I had planned on guests spending several hours at the table. So even if we didn't have the clientele to turn a table, at least it would be occupied for most of the night, creating the illusion that the restaurant was always busy.

Now, rather than have a few tables sit vacant all night, we simply removed the extra tables. We also started taking reservations back to back. So if you came in at 7:30, there would be a table seated next you with 6:30 reservations. When they were finished, an 8:30 reservation would take their place. So even if we only had 20 reservations, you would get the feeling you were in a busy restaurant. Thankfully, as time passed and the restaurant became more popular, we no longer had to hide tables.

For the first two years, neither Melissa or I made a cent. Everything the restaurant took in went to employee payroll and paying off our massive debt, which, when all was said and done, was well over a million dollars. They were tough times for sure, but we made it through together.

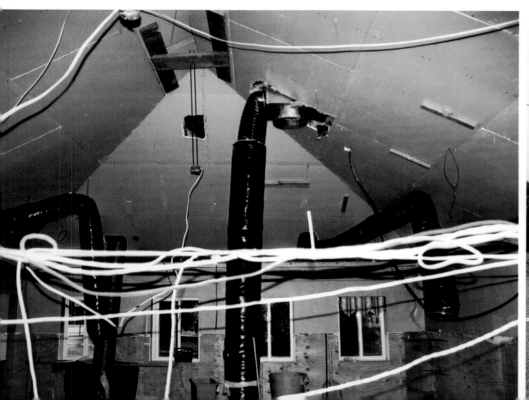

We were nearly out of the woods, or so we thought. When it was time to do our taxes, we wound up owing around $70,000. I didn't think that was possible since Melissa and I made no money. It all went to paying off those damn cards. What I didn't realize then was that that money was still considered income. It was just another one of the rookie mistakes I made in the early years. We had to take out yet another credit card just to square off our taxes. It took some time, but eventually we made peace with the IRS.

When the bills were all paid off, we got rid of the renters and reclaimed our house. We even bought a new car. As for the Probe, I gave it to one of my employees, still with a shot clutch and a broken headlight.

In 2005, the restaurant went under more renovations. One of my top priorities was to warm up the dining room. Although most loyal customers had no real issue with the modest décor, the upgrade was not for them. It was for the person eating a well-done steak and a green salad. My reasoning was that this person is never going to think that my restaurant is anything but average. You can get a well-done steak and a green salad anywhere. And whether it's at Restaurant Nicholas or Applebee's, it's basically going to taste the same. If the experience is special, if the service transcends typical, then the person eating a well-done steak and a green salad will think that it was the best well-done steak and green salad they had ever eaten. If I can make a picky or less adventurous eater have a superb dining experience, then I really have done my job.

Now we're not rivaling the extreme luxury of the St. Regis Hotel or the old Lespinasse, but for a small owner-operated restaurant in suburban New Jersey, we offer a unique experience that is tough to find outside the city. When you walk through the doors of Restaurant Nicholas, you are immediately consumed by its lavish ambiance. From the marble floors and the hand-blown glass chandelier to the sophisticated lounge and elegant wine list, you feel like you are about to embark on something special.

JULIANA LAYLA, "WON'T YOU EASE MY WORRIED MIND?"

It took a great deal of perseverance and some trial and error to create the establishment that stands today. Thanks to my staff, specifically the ones who have stuck it out for many years, Restaurant Nicholas has matured into a destination rather than just some place to eat.

The daily grind of running this place has gotten a little easier as time has passed. Just like spinning pizzas was wired into

my nervous system all those years ago, running a restaurant has become second nature. Much of the weight has been relieved by some key members of my staff, and for that, I am grateful.

Don't get the wrong impression, though. This job still isn't easy. There is a new obstacle to overcome every day. Whether it's equipment breaking or line cooks taking a permanent vacation, I need to always prepare for the worst. I try to keep this rigid outlook separate from my personal life, so I can be a little sunnier with Melissa and little Nicholas. Easier said than done.

So on the morning of July 15, 2009, I'm trying not to think about the restaurant. I'm trying desperately to channel my thoughts to a happier place, keeping a grasp on that sunny outlook. Melissa is once again in the maternity ward of Riverview Hospital. Unfortunately, I am not there with her. I'm in the lobby arguing with three lawyers.

Some papers needed to be signed and notarized, and though I insisted that this matter be squared away by early July so I could focus on the birth of my second child uninterrupted, circumstance and Murphy's Law brought us here: in a hospital lobby at 7:05 a.m. Needless to say, I lose my cool and create somewhat of a scene. Can you blame me? My wife is being prepped to give birth and still nothing but business on my end. Some things never change.

After a small tug of war, the papers are finally signed. Upon their exit, the lawyers all wish me luck with the delivery. Yeah, thanks guys….

Now a little edgy, I go back to where I really needed to be: with my wife. For the first time that morning, my thoughts are now focused on the moment.

Juliana Layla Harary was born that morning, healthy and beautiful. The birth of Juliana was amazing, just how I remembered when little Nicholas was born, only I didn't have to dart back to the restaurant. Little Nicholas now had a little sister. I now had a daughter. And Melissa and I had a little family.

In my pocket, my cellphone buzzes. I immediately fear the worst. I take a deep, calming breath. "Please don't be the restaurant," I chant repeatedly in my head. The tiny monitor on my phone reads "MANNY," my current chef de cuisine. My blood runs even colder.

Was it a fire or another flood, I think? Did my entire kitchen

crew get arrested? Damn, I knew that would happen one of these days. I've spent the last nine years tackling dilemmas of all shapes and sizes. I answer the phone with apprehension and a quick and brusque "Yeah?"

"Hey, Nicholas, how are you and Melissa doing? Just calling to wish you luck."

There are no fires or floods. No one was arrested.

I had expected the worst with Manny's phone call. It may seem a little pessimistic, but that's how I stay sane in my insane world. After a busy Saturday night, we may receive upwards of 60 comment cards from guests, 59 of which could be positive. But it's the one negative comment that I'll spend my Sunday thinking about. It's rarely about what went right but what went wrong that sticks in my head the following day.

I feel good knowing that my children will have a much happier childhood than I did. I hope their outlook on life will be a bit more pleasant than mine. Oddly, had I not had the tough childhood I did, I may have taken a much different route in life. So I guess there was a bright side to it all. That fire that was lit inside me years ago still burns, and always will. My sister often makes the joke, "Nicholas has some serious issues, but his issues make him very successful." Perhaps when I retire I will seek some professional help.

Having spoken to many chefs and restaurateurs, I came to the conclusion that my perception on life isn't unique. These men and women all have serious control issues sprinkled with a healthy dose of obsessive-compulsive disorder. Perhaps that's the reason why we're all in a business which requires extreme dedication and an immense amount of attention to detail.

Reflecting on how Melissa and I got this restaurant off the ground, I'm amazed that, despite my naïveté, I never once doubted that we wouldn't be successful. I'm often asked, "Can this be done again?" It's a difficult question because the answer depends on several conditions.

The short answer is "No." It can't be done again, at least not the same way we did it. Much has changed in nine years, and the moves we pulled probably won't work now. I sometimes laugh out loud remembering how crazy the early years were. The story of how we opened Restaurant Nicholas is so unbelievable, you would have to be crazy to try to replicate it. And if you do try, good luck. You will need it.

Many talented young cooks come and go through my kitchen. A few aspire to open their own businesses. Whether it's a deli or a catering hall or the next four-star restaurant in suburban New Jersey, I try to help them as much as I can. I also give it to them straight: the odds of succeeding in the restaurant business are pretty slim. I'm not trying to discourage anyone; I would love to see a current or former employee reach their ultimate goal, but it's not easy. The dedication involved in opening a restaurant is nothing short of life consuming. I'm living proof of that!

If you are dedicated, if you have passion, and if you're crazy enough to attempt it in the first place, then the answer to that question is, "Yes, it can be done again." Anything is possible, regardless of your upbringing or financial status. If you work hard, stay focused and persevere, you will get results. The transformation from an idea to a successful restaurant took many years and many trips to the drawing board. The required time and effort can never be compromised, otherwise you risk being just another casualty of the business.

Perhaps one day Melissa and I will begin another project. For now, I am really enjoying my time as a family man. Little Nicholas is getting bigger. I bring him into the kitchen every now and then. He seems to be really intrigued. I'm not prepping the little guy to be the next chef, but I think it's important for him to see early on how hard people in this industry work. As for Juliana, it's a new chapter in my life, one which I wholeheartedly welcome. Perhaps what I missed as a kid I can relive through my children. I don't know. What I do know is I have a beautiful family, not just with Melissa and the kids, but also my family at the restaurant, as dysfunctional as we may be.

August 2009

Life on the Line

Thanks to the media, chefs have grown in popularity in recent years. It appears that being a chef these days is quite hip and even glamorous. You've seen the shows, different chefs and cooks making food, having a good time, and playing for the camera. Although cooking professionally certainly can be fun, the dedication is more disciplined and the work is much harder than most people realize.

To want to be a chef takes a special breed. Talk to any one of my kitchen crew and you'll quickly realize that you're not dealing with ordinary people. The hours are long. The work is hard. The sweating is continuous. Cuts and burns are commonplace. Working weekends and holidays are a given. The pay isn't all that great. Three out of four new cooks won't make it past six months. If any of these occupational "perks" seem unreasonable, then I suggest you seek employment elsewhere.

Besides having a passion for their craft, a chef or line cook in this caliber of restaurant needs to be extremely focused throughout the day. Every minute is accounted for. If a single one goes by when you don't care and half-ass a project, it could inevitably affect someone's dinner later that evening. The food has to be the best it can be, otherwise a guest may think their meal was only okay, or worse yet, awful. Unacceptable. Good cooks understand this and strive to put out the best food possible.

A busy Saturday night is like a symphony. Skilled cooks throughout the kitchen fire up as many as a half dozen tables at once, resulting in plumes of smoke and a cacophony of clanging pots and pans. Then, out of the chaos, table by table, the dishes elegantly emerge. The meat dishes timed perfectly with the fish. The salads, made at the last minute so they don't wilt, coinciding with steaming bowls of pasta. Then all the plates are scrupulously examined. Was it seasoned enough? Did you taste the sauce? Was the fish overcooked? Undercooked? Every aspect is taken into account.

Timing and precision are everything. When all is going well, the kitchen runs like a well-oiled machine. However, if just one cook on one dish misses the mark, it can throw off the kitchen's entire rhythm, and the next hour or so will be spent trying to muscle out of the "weeds."

When dinner service is over—and, for better or worse, it will eventually be over—the whole kitchen needs to be cleaned. The stoves get scrubbed, the floors get mopped, and the stainless steel countertops get polished. Don't wait for compliments or pats on the back when the night is through, either. This is what's expected of you. If you're going to get any feedback, more often than not it will be negative.

Then why do we do it? Why would anyone put up with all of that for a salary comparable to a Starbucks barista? For us, there's a personal satisfaction that comes from being your best, day in and day out. It's being able to accomplish something that might have seemed impossible hours ago. It's impressing people and making them appreciate what all those hours, blood, sweat and tears were for. And perhaps it's knowing that we do what not many other people could do that keeps us showing up for work the next morning.

How to Use This Book

In today's fast-paced world, we are all too familiar with 30-minute meals and quick, easy dinners.

Although some of the recipes in this book lean towards easy, most can be quite challenging and time consuming. Be sure to read the entire recipe first, so you know what you're getting into. The Braised Suckling Pig on page 136, for example, takes three days to complete—probably not the best one to choose when your dinner guests are to arrive in less than two hours.

Use the recipes as guidelines and mine them for ideas. While braising the pig may be out of the question, the Parsnip Puree and Poached Quince that accompany the pig might go perfectly with the pork chops you were planning to make.

Some of the techniques used in these recipes might require some practice before you get them right. No matter how well we try to explain a procedure, much of cooking is about look and feel. It's not an exact science. Making pasta dough or an emulsified butter sauce, for example, might be second nature to my cooks in the restaurant, but if you've never made them before, it might not be so effortless. If you nail the Hen Egg Ravioli the first time, you're a better cook than me.

Most importantly, use common sense. You're not going to find fresh corn in New Jersey in February. And if you can, it probably won't be that great. If a recipe says to cook a fish fillet four minutes, but it appears done in three, then it probably is. If a piece of meat is turning black, then it's probably burning.

These dishes take time, patience and a little love. I hope they bring you and your friends as much joy as they've brought me and the guests of Restaurant Nicholas. When completing a successful dinner, you should feel a sense of accomplishment that simply cannot be obtained in 30 minutes. Enjoy.

SOME OTHER GROUND RULES TO CONSIDER:
Use heavy-bottomed pots and pans. If you do not own any, get some. It's worth the price. They distribute the heat evenly, preventing your food from scorching on one half and being undercooked on the other. At the restaurant, we use black steel pans, which resemble cast iron, though good quality stainless steel or copper pans are acceptable.

Mis en place, which translates into put in place. In other words, have all your tools and ingredients organized before starting a recipe.

Several recipes call for sauces and vinaigrettes to be emulsified, which refers the molecules of fat (butter, oil, etc.) being suspended in a liquid (water, egg yolk,

stock, etc.). The result is a creamy looking product with a uniform consistency. If done improperly, your sauce will "break" into two separate parts (think oil and vinegar).

After cooking, meat should be allowed to "rest" at room temperature for a few minutes. This allows the juices, which have been pushed to the outside from the cooking process, to be reabsorbed. If a steak is sliced right out of the oven, all the juices will run out, leaving the meat dry.

For some recipes, a convection oven is preferred for hotter, drier cooking. If you don't own a convection oven, a conventional oven set 50 degrees higher than specified can be substituted.

If a unit of measure isn't specified for an ingredient, it's assumed to be used as much as needed (oil for deep frying, bench flour, etc.) or to taste (salt and pepper).

Many recipes require you to sweat vegetables, which means cooking them slow and low in a minimal amount of fat (butter, oil, etc.). You don't want the vegetables to caramelize or pick up any color.

Deglazing is the process of releasing the caramelized bits of meat or vegetables stuck to the bottom of a pan by adding a liquid (wine, vinegar, water, etc.) to the hot pan and loosening the bits with a spoon. They may not look like much, but those bits pack a lot of punch and will intensify the flavor of your soups and sauces.

All butter used is unsalted, so we can control the amount of salt in a dish. We like to use sea salt in the restaurant. Kosher salt is also acceptable. For finishing, I like large-grain salt, like *fleur de sel* or *sel gris*.

All herbs are fresh unless otherwise specified. All pepper is freshly ground.

Mirepoix, or root vegetables such carrots, onions and celery root, are always peeled unless otherwise noted.

Special Equipment

TAMIS Also known as a drum sieve. Used to achieve a very smooth consistency of whipped potatoes and dense purees. It can also be used to sift flour.

CHINOIS Professional-grade, fine-mesh conical strainer used for soups, sauces and loose purees. The mesh is much finer in a chinois than a conventional strainer, allowing for a smooth, velvety product.

BLENDER Of all the tools used at the restaurant, this is one of the most important. You do not need a professional-grade blender, such as a Vita Prep, which will run you about $500, though if you're serious about cooking, it's a good investment. If solid foods won't puree in your blender, try putting them in your food processor first. When pureeing hot liquids, do not fill the blender more than halfway. The liquid's volume will increase as it purees. I can tell you from experience, you do not want a face full of hot soup.

CHEF'S KNIFE I'm not going to tell you to purchase a $300 hand-crafted Japanese blade—they are pretty cool, though—just make sure your knife is razor sharp. It will make your life easier and your cuts more precise. It's also a lot safer than a dull knife.

SHARPENING STEEL A big misconception is that this tool sharpens knives. Instead, it keeps your knife sharp by keeping the edge of the blade straight. If you're doing a lot of chopping, a few strokes on the steel will prolong the sharpness of your knife.

SHEET PANS When we refer to sheet pans in this book, we are actually referring to half sheet pans (in technical jargon). Full sheet pans will not fit into most home refrigerators. Cookie sheets can be used, but sheet pans are heavier and will last longer. Any kitchen supply store will carry them.

CAKE TESTER A thin wire attached to a plastic handle also used to test the doneness of fish. Pierce the widest part of the fillet with the tester and hold for a few seconds. Check the temperature of the wire on your bottom lip. If the metal is still cold, the fish isn't done. You want it to be just warm. If the tester is hot, your fish is overcooked.

MANDOLINE Used for juliennes or paper-thin slices. I prefer the cheaper, plastic Japanese version to the big, steel French ones, which are clunky and expensive. I have seen more accidents with a mandoline than any other tool; I have the scars to prove it.

PARCHMENT PAPER Great for baking. It's heatproof, mostly nonstick, protects your bakeware and makes for an easy clean-up.

DEEP FRYER Electric deep fryers for the home are safer, cleaner and more accurate than a pot of hot oil on the stovetop. If you are going to set up your own fryer, be cautious. Use a heavy-bottomed pot and a heat-resistant thermometer. Do not fill the pot more than halfway; the volume of the oil will expand when something is placed in it. 325-degree oil flowing into an open flame is not a great thing. Hot oil splashing on your skin sucks. Really, just buy a deep fryer.

VACUUM SEAL MACHINE If you plan on using the "sous vide" method, this tool is invaluable. Foodsaver makes a reputable product costing around $150. It's also good for storing or freezing foods.

IMMERSION THERMAL CIRCULATOR Used to achieve and maintain the temperature of a hot water bath for sous vide cooking. They are available at kitchen supply stores like JB Prince for nearly $1000. In the book, I will explain how to sous vide without one.

Knife Cuts

LARGE DICE ¾ inch cubed.

MEDIUM DICE ½ inch cubed.

SMALL DICE ¼ inch cubed.

BRUNOIS ⅛ inch cubed.

FINE BRUNOIS ¹⁄₁₆ inch cubed.

MINCED Very small bits, smaller than the smallest dice; not uniform.

ROUGH CHOP Approximately 1-inch pieces; not uniform; mostly used for items that will be discarded (stock vegetables) or pureed.

BATONNET ½ inch square by 2 ½ – 3 inches.

JULIENNE ⅛ inch square by 2 ½ – 3 inches.

CONCASSE Primarily refers to tomatoes, whose skin and seeds are removed.

CHIFFONADE Very thin strands of herbs or leaves.

BIAS Diagonal cuts, usually for thin loaves of bread, scallions, etc.

SUPREMES Citrus segments cleaned of membrane and seeds. To produce supremes, remove the top and bottom of the fruit. Cut away the skin and any white pith, slicing from top to bottom. Cut out the supreme segments between each membrane.

Asian Beef Tartare Consommé Serves Eight

INGREDIENTS

Consommé

3 quarts Chicken Stock (see
  page 227)
¾ cup light soy sauce
1 bunch scallions, chopped
3 cloves garlic, chopped
2 tablespoons ginger, chopped
1 teaspoon sesame oil
2 cups egg whites
8 ounces boneless, skinless
  chicken breast, chopped

Beef Tartare

20 ounces beef tenderloin, finely
  chopped
½ tablespoon scallions, white part
  only, minced
½ tablespoon cilantro, julienne
1 tablespoon jalapeno, brunoise
½ teaspoon sesame seeds, lightly
  toasted
1 teaspoon soy sauce
1 tablespoon daikon radish,
  brunoise
1½ cups wonton wrapper,
  julienne
1 quart vegetable oil (for frying)
¼ cup scallion greens, thinly
  sliced on the bias (for garnish)
Salt and pepper

CONSOMMÉ (YIELDS 1½ QUARTS)

In a food processor, combine scallions, garlic, ginger and egg whites. When the egg whites begin to froth, add the chicken. Continue processing until a smooth, frothy mixture develops.

Add the stock, chicken mixture, soy sauce and sesame oil to a large, heavy-bottomed pot. Gently mix all ingredients together and bring to a boil. Reduce heat to a low simmer. From this point do not stir. The egg whites will coagulate and rise to the surface, forming a "raft" that will clarify the stock. Make a small hole approximately 3 or 4 inches in diameter in the center of the raft to allow the simmering stock to bubble up and wash over the raft. Simmer the consommé for 30 minutes then remove from heat.

Through the hole in the raft, gently ladle the broth through a fine-mesh strainer. The consommé should be a dark, translucent amber color. Let it cool and refrigerate.

Note: The consommé can be made in advance and refrigerated for up to 3 days or frozen for 4 months.

BEEF TARTARE

Set the deep fryer to 325 degrees or heat the oil to that temperature over medium heat in a large, heavy-bottomed pot (use a candy thermometer to check the temperature). It is very important to have a large pot because when the wontons are added, the oil will bubble up and rise quickly. Carefully add the wonton strips to the oil and fry until golden and crispy, about 30–45 seconds. Remove the strips from the oil using a slotted spoon and drain on paper towels. Season with salt and reserve.

In a large bowl, fold together the beef, soy sauce, minced scallions, jalapeno, cilantro, sesame seeds and daikon. Season with salt and pepper.

ASSEMBLY

Place a 2½-inch ring mold in the center of a serving bowl. Pack the mold tightly with the tartare and carefully remove the mold. Garnish with the green scallions and fried wontons. Pour the desired amount of consommé over and around the tartare.

NOTES

SPECIAL EQUIPMENT: 2½-inch ring mold, chinois or fine-mesh strainer, deep fryer (optional).

 WINE PAIRING: Floral Alsatian Gewürztraminers stand up nicely to these Asian flavors. Choose a wine with a hint of sweetness.

The crunchy wonton strips are essential to this dish. A good beef tartare needs to be layered with varying textures, otherwise it will only have a single dimension on your palate. If you want to avoid deep frying, a store-bought sesame noodle can be substituted.

Crosnes are small, pale tubers native to China and Japan, where they are considered a sign of good luck. Whether eaten raw or cooked, their flavor is similar to that of Jerusalem artichokes or sunchokes.

Pickled Beet Salad with Crosnes Serves Eight

Although not the easiest to find, crosnes, which are sometimes called knot root or chorogi (Japanese for "longevity"), have recently grown in popularity. Check high-end farmers markets or Asian markets. They can also be ordered online. In this dish, they add a crunchy texture to the softer beets. If crosnes are not available, walnuts can be substituted.

PICKLING LIQUID (YIELDS 1 QUART)
Place all ingredients except for the parsley and thyme in a large pot and bring to a boil. Reduce heat and simmer for 45 minutes. Remove pot from heat, add fresh herbs, and let steep for 1 hour. Strain.

ROASTED BEETS
Preheat oven to 425 degrees. Remove and discard any stems from the beets.

When roasting beets, it is important to keep each variety separate otherwise their vibrant colors may bleed into each other. Beginning with the yellow beets, toss them in oil, season with salt, and wrap tightly in foil. Repeat with chiogas, then reds.

Place foil packs on a sheet pan and roast on the middle oven rack for 30 minutes. Check the smaller beets for doneness by inserting a paring knife through the center of one of the beets. If it pierces through with no resistance, the beets are done. Check every 15 minutes until all of the beets are done. Remove from foil and let cool for at least 1 hour.

With a pair of rubber gloves and a kitchen towel, remove the outer layer of skin. Cut the larger beets into quarters and the smaller ones into halves. Place each variety of beets into separate containers and cover with warm pickling liquid. Let cool on countertop then refrigerate.

Note: When roasting beets, the window between underdone and overdone is very small. Keep in mind that the larger the beet, the longer it will take to cook. At the restaurant, the beets are separated into large and small categories. Pickled beets have a shelf life of over a year.

CROSNES
Remove the fibrous ends from each crosne. In a bowl, toss the crosnes with salt. The crosnes will start to exude moisture. Rinse in cold water and repeat two more times. Let dry. Pickle the raw crosnes the same way as the beets.

ASSEMBLY
Remove the bottom stem from each head of frisee. With a pair of kitchen shears, trim the frisee into bite-size pieces. Thoroughly wash in cold water and dry in a salad spinner.

Toss the frisee with 1 tablespoon of the pickling liquid, salt and pepper. Place 1 cup of dressed frisee in the center of the plate. Alternate beets and crosnes around the frisee. Drizzle with olive oil.

NOTES
WINE PAIRING: The Marches region of Italy, located on the Adriatic Coast, is a bountiful culinary area with incredible produce. The local white wine, Verdicchio, is a high tone, vibrant wine with plenty of acidity—perfect for the pickled beets.

INGREDIENTS

Pickling Liquid
1 quart apple cider vinegar
1 tablespoon salt
1 clove garlic, chopped
1 shallot, chopped
2 tablespoons coriander seed
2 tablespoons fennel seed
1 Thai chili
1 bay leaf
5 sprigs parsley
5 sprigs thyme
¼ cup sugar

Roasted Beets
4 small red beets (approximately 1 pound)
4 small yellow beets (approximately 1 pound)
8 small chioga beets (approximately 1 pound)
3 tablespoons grapeseed oil
Salt

Crosnes
½ cup crosnes (approximately 8 ounces)
¼ cup coarse or kosher salt

Salad
4 heads of frisee

Crab Salad with Gazpacho Sorbet *Serves Eight*

INGREDIENTS

Gazpacho Sorbet

2 ripe plum tomatoes, rough
   chopped
1 red pepper, rough chopped
1 English cucumber, peeled,
   seeded and rough chopped
½ clove garlic, minced
½ shallot, minced
¼ cup sugar
¼ cup red wine vinegar
Stabilizer sevagel (optional)
Salt and pepper

Sherry Mayonnaise

1 egg yolk
2 cups salad oil (such as canola
   or vegetable), slightly chilled
⅓ cup sherry vinegar
Salt and pepper

Crab Salad

4 cups super lump crabmeat
¼ cup tomato, concasse and
   small dice
¼ cup avocado, small dice,
   tossed in lemon juice
¼ cup English cucumber, skin
   on, seeded, small dice
1 tablespoon parsley, chopped
¼ cup Sherry Mayonnaise
Salt and pepper
2 tablespoons chives, finely
   chopped

GAZPACHO SORBET

Combine the vegetables, sugar and vinegar in a blender and puree until smooth. Adjust the seasoning with salt and pepper. Pass the puree through a chinois and discard the solids. Weigh the puree in grams. The amount of sorbet stabilizer will be 1 percent of the weight of the puree (500 grams of puree will equal 5 grams of stabilizer).

Heat 1 cup of puree on the stovetop. When it comes to a boil, combine it with the measured stabilizer in a mixing bowl and whisk to eliminate any lumps. Reintroduce the cup of stabilized product into the remaining puree.

In a medium-sized pot, bring the puree back to a boil, whisking constantly. Remove from the heat and let cool. Spin the puree in an ice cream machine using the manufacturer's instructions. Freeze until needed. Ideally, this should be done a few hours before serving.

SHERRY MAYONNAISE

Place the egg yolk in a food processor. With the blade running on high, slowly drizzle in the oil. When all of the oil has been incorporated, add the sherry vinegar. Adjust the seasoning with salt and pepper. Refrigerate until needed.

ASSEMBLY

Remove the sorbet from the freezer about 10 minutes before serving to allow it to soften.

Combine the crabmeat, parsley and vegetables in a bowl. Add the mayonnaise and gently fold it all together with a spoon. Adjust the seasoning with salt and pepper. Spoon ½ cup of the crab salad into a 2½-inch mold. (At the restaurant, we use a square mold, however a round mold will work just as well.)

Spoon a quenelle or small scoop of the sorbet atop each salad. Garnish the sorbet with chopped chives.

NOTES

SPECIAL EQUIPMENT: Chinois or fine-mesh strainer, ice cream machine, 2½-inch ring mold.

 WINE PAIRING: It's somewhat difficult to pair a wine with gazpacho's intense tomato flavor. An Austrian Grüner Veltliner's unique combination of fruit, minerality and acidity should stand up to the tomato.

This is one of my favorite summertime appetizers. If you do not have an ice cream machine, the gazpacho can be used as a sauce. Just make sure it is ice cold.

This salad is built around Beufort cheese. Beufort is a village on the border of Switzerland and France. The cows there graze on pastures filled with hazelnut flowers, giving their milk a mildly nutty flavor.

Green Salad with Candied
Hazelnuts and Beaufort Cheese Serves Eight

Besides complementing the cheese, the candied hazelnuts in the salad offer sweet and crunchy elements that offset the vinaigrette's tartness. This is one of the few dishes on the menu all year round.

If you decide not to candy your own hazelnuts, any store-bought candied nuts can be substituted.

CANDIED HAZELNUTS

Preheat the oven to 350 degrees. Place the hazelnuts on a sheet pan and toast for 10 minutes. Transfer the nuts to a large bowl and toss them with the lime juice and cayenne. Return the nuts to the oven and toast for an additional 8 minutes.

Add the sugar to a large heavy-bottomed pot. Cook on medium heat, continuously stirring with a wooden spoon. When the sugar begins to melt and caramelize, lower the heat. Stir in the butter after all the sugar granules have melted into a light brown syrup. Fold in the hazelnuts to coat them in the caramel. Be careful. The caramelized sugar is extremely hot.

Spoon out the nuts on a sheet pan lined with a Silpat. Then individually transfer each nut to another sheet pan lined with a Silpat in order to prevent the nuts from sticking together. It is important to work quickly. The caramelized sugar will begin to cool and harden, making it difficult to separate the nuts.

Let the hazelnuts cool completely. Agitate them with your hands to release any nuts that have stuck together. Cut each nut in half and store in a cool, dry place.

HAZELNUT VINAIGRETTE

Whisk the oils and vinegar together. Season with salt and pepper, and refrigerate until needed. Shake the vinaigrette before serving.

ASSEMBLY

Slice the cheese into thin strips using a vegetable peeler. Cut the apricots into thick strips.

In a large bowl, toss a portion of greens with approximately ¼ cup of the vinaigrette. Season with salt and pepper. Stack the greens high on a serving plate. Lean 4 or 5 slices of the cheese around the greens. Sprinkle the hazelnuts and the apricots around the perimeter of the salad and serve.

NOTES

SPECIAL EQUIPMENT: 2 Silpats or other silicone baking sheets.

WINE PAIRING: Salads dressed with vinaigrette are hard to pair with wine. A crisp elegant glass of Champagne, however, should do the trick.

INGREDIENTS

Candied Hazelnuts
2 cups hazelnuts, shelled
Juice of 1 lime
Pinch of cayenne pepper
1½ cups sugar
½ teaspoon butter

Hazelnut Vinaigrette
½ cup hazelnut oil
½ cup olive oil
½ cup red wine vinegar
Salt and pepper

Salad
1½ pounds field green mix
8 ounces Beaufort cheese
1 cup dried apricots
Salt and pepper

Lobster Caviar with Cucumber Gelée Serves Eight

This was one of our most popular dishes at the restaurant. Although this recipe is quite stylish, it was merely created with ingredients that were on hand. We had a few empty caviar tins kicking around, so I thought it would be cool to use them as serving vessels for a caviar dish. We originally tried the recipe with crabmeat but found the flavors of the crab and caviar got lost within each other. We tried it with lobster and had great results. The cucumber gelée not only adds a refreshing layer, it helps the caviar spread evenly on top of the lobster. At the restaurant we mold the gelée into a thin circle that sits on top of the lobster. This is a project in itself, therefore we modified this aspect of the recipe for the home cook. Keep in mind one of the main points of this presentation is to create the illusion that there is a full container of caviar. When your guests break into the top layer, they will be surprised to see lobster hiding underneath. This can also be done in a larger format for cocktail parties.

INGREDIENTS

Cucumber Gelée
1 large cucumber
1 sheet gelatin, 3 x 8 inches
Pinch of sugar
Pinch of salt

Lobster Caviar
2 cups cooked lobster meat,
  rough chopped
¼ cup cucumber, small dice
¼ cup red onion, small dice
¼ cup chives, finely chopped
⅓ cup crème fraîche
½ tablespoon lemon juice
1½ tablespoons extra-virgin
  olive oil
8 ounces caviar
½ cup Cucumber Gelée
16 slices brioche, quartered into
  triangles and toasted
Salt

CUCUMBER GELÉE
Place the gelatin sheet into a bowl of cold water to "bloom." After about 5 minutes, it should be very soft and ready to use.

Peel the cucumber and cut it into pieces. Pass the pieces through the juicer to yield ½ cup of cucumber juice. Season the juice with sugar and salt.

Combine the cucumber juice and gelatin in a small saucepot and heat on low until the gelatin is completely melted, stirring occasionally. Transfer the cucumber juice to a small bowl and refrigerate for at least 2 hours to set.

When the gelée is set, break it apart with a spoon so it resembles something like a jam.

LOBSTER CAVIAR
Combine the first 5 ingredients in a small bowl. Separately, whisk together the lemon juice and olive oil and gently mix it into the lobster salad. Season with salt.

ASSEMBLY
Spoon the salad into the ramekins, leaving about ¼ inch at the top. Spread 1 tablespoon of the gelée on top. With a plastic spoon carefully spread 1 ounce of caviar over the gelée. Serve with toasted brioche triangles.

NOTES
SPECIAL EQUIPMENT: 8 2½-inch ramekins, electric fruit/vegetable juicer.

 WINE PAIRING: What else but Champagne could complement such a luxurious dish? All decadence aside, the acidity and carbonation of Champagne, or any sparkling white wine, cuts through the richness of the caviar, allowing it to have a purer taste.

We use hackleback sturgeon caviar for this dish. It is milder than beluga or osetra and priced around $40 per ounce, as opposed to $100 per ounce.

If you attempt this dish, try it with the caviar. You'll be surprised at how perfect the flavors go together.

Pickled Oysters Serves Eight

Being close to the Jersey Shore, I wanted some type of oyster dish on the menu. But I also wanted something that separated us from so many of the "oysters on the half shell" appetizers found on other menus. Typically, raw oysters are served with a mignonette. What would happen if you infused the mignonette into the oyster, in essence pickling them?

We tried a few different vinegars and techniques until we reached what we have today. A small quenelle of crème fraîche rounded out the flavors. It was good, if not entirely elegant, so I thought a small dollop of caviar would bring it over the top.

The people who ordered the dish raved about it. However, we didn't sell all that many. I knew oysters were popular in most fine-dining restaurants, especially ones near the ocean, so why wasn't our dish selling like I expected? Apparently, the caveat was caviar. Once I took it off the dish, people immediately started ordering the oysters. Occasionally, we still have old-school customers order the oysters with caviar.

Thoroughly rinse the oysters 2–3 times. Shuck each oyster. Place the meat into a bowl and reserve the top half of each shell.

Boil the empty shells in a large pot of boiling water for 15 minutes. Strain. Scrub each shell with an abrasive sponge to remove any muscle attached to the inside. Rinse and allow to dry.

Reserve 1 cup of the oyster liquor that gathered in the bowl. Run cold water over the bowl of oysters to remove any pieces of shell or dirt. Strain the oysters and refrigerate until ready to use.

In a large pot, heat the vinegar, sugar, peppercorns, star anise, cloves, and carrot and fennel trim. Simmer for 10 minutes and strain. Discard the solids. Bring the liquid to a boil in a clean pot, add the brunoise carrot and fennel, and cook for 10 seconds. Pour the hot liquid directly over the bowl of oysters. Return the bowl to the refrigerator to completely chill.

ASSEMBLY
Place the oysters back into the clean shells. Garnish with a small dollop of crème fraîche, minced onion and chives. Serve 6 oysters per person.

NOTES
WINE PAIRING: At the restaurant, the house vodka is an incredibly smooth Russian selection called Zyr. Served ice cold, it's the perfect match for oysters.

INGREDIENTS

1 quart rice wine vinegar

1 cup sugar

2 teaspoons Szechuan peppercorns

5 whole star anise

3 whole cloves

½ cup carrots, brunoise, trim reserved plus more to yield an additional cup

½ cup fennel, brunoise, trim reserved plus more to yield an additional cup

4 dozen oysters

1 cup crème fraîche

½ cup red onion, minced

½ cup chives, finely chopped

Poached Florida Gulf
Shrimp with Horseradish Consommé Serves Eight

This dish was created for my high school friend David Katz, the creator of Zyr vodka. He wanted me to come up with a dish to accompany his vodka. Since it's common to see a Bloody Mary garnished with a piece of poached shrimp, I played with that concept. I eventually ended up with a lighter, more modern approach to shrimp cocktail.

INGREDIENTS

Horseradish Consommé
15 ripe plum tomatoes, quartered
2 tablespoons salt
3 tablespoons sugar
¼ cup fresh horseradish, grated

Shrimp
48 shrimp (16–18 size), cleaned
1 gallon Court Bouillon (see
  page 228)
½ cup grape tomatoes, halved
½ English cucumber
¼ cup chives, finely chopped
1 tablespoon extra-virgin olive oil
1 teaspoon lemon juice
1 bunch mâche, leaves washed
  and dried
Coarse salt and white pepper

HORSERADISH CONSOMMÉ
Puree the tomatoes, salt and sugar in a blender until the mixture is completely smooth. Line a chinois or fine-mesh strainer with a cloth napkin and place it over a deep pot. Pour the tomato mixture into the chinois. Place the pot in the refrigerator overnight. The liquid from the tomatoes will strain through the napkin leaving a clear, light pink liquid.

The following day, remove the pot from the refrigerator and discard the tomato pulp. Stir the grated horseradish into the liquid and let it steep for 2 hours. Strain.

ASSEMBLY
Peel the cucumber and scoop out tiny balls with the Parisian scoop or melon baller. Be sure to scoop only the flesh not the seeds. Reserve.

Bring the Court Bouillon to a boil in a large pot then reduce it to a simmer. Working in batches, add the shrimp to the bouillon and cook for 2 minutes. Transfer the cooked shrimp to a large ice bath to stop the cooking process. Drain well on paper towels. Repeat the process with the remaining shrimp.

Pick out 8 of the nicest shrimp for the garnish. Butterfly each shrimp by slicing it in half horizontally, leaving the tail intact. Open the shrimp halves like a book. Reserve.

Cut the rest of the shrimp into thirds or fourths, depending on the size, and toss them with the olive oil, lemon juice and chives. Season with salt and pepper.

Spoon approximately ⅓ cup of the chopped shrimp into the center of a bowl. Place the butterflied shrimp directly on top. Arrange the tomatoes and cucumber balls around the perimeter of the shrimp. Ladle ½ cup of horseradish consommé around the shrimp and garnish with a few leaves of mâche. For a more elegant presentation, you could garnish the shrimp first and ladle the consommé tableside.

NOTES
SPECIAL EQUIPMENT: Chinois or fine-mesh strainer, Parisian scoop or melon baller.

 WINE PAIRING: The clean, streamlined flavor of the consommé is an ideal match with the minerality of an Austrian Sauvignon Blanc.

This is a great summer dish and very easy to do. Its elegant presentation is sure to impress your guests.

Seafood Tasting:
Crab Salad with Mango and Tomato-Basil Vinaigrette Serves Eight

Note: This recipe is part of the Seafood Tasting set of recipes, which serves eight.

TOMATO-BASIL VINAIGRETTE

In a medium saucepot, heat ¼ cup of the olive oil on medium-low heat. Sweat the garlic and shallots in the oil, about 8 minutes. Add the tomatoes. Season with salt and pepper and cook for 40 minutes, stirring periodically. Deglaze the pot with ¼ cup of the vinegar and cook for an additional 5 minutes. Transfer the tomatoes to a bowl and refrigerate.

When the tomatoes have cooled, place them in a blender with the remaining vinegar, basil and sugar. Blend on high and slowly drizzle the remaining olive oil into the tomatoes. Adjust the seasoning with salt and pepper. Strain the vinaigrette through a chinois and refrigerate until needed.

CRAB SALAD

Carefully pick through the crab to remove any bits of shell. For a more thorough search, place the crab under a black light. The bits of shell will glow bright white.

Transfer the crab to a bowl and fold in the remaining ingredients. Season with salt and pepper. Garnish with additional chive batons, if desired.

NOTES
SPECIAL EQUIPMENT: Chinois or fine-mesh strainer.

 WINE PAIRING: Pair this dish with a crisp Champagne, such as a Blanc de Blancs, especially if you serve it as a first course. Its acidity and effervescence cleanse the palate, allowing you to fully experience the three distinct flavors in this dish. It also makes for an elegant presentation.

INGREDIENTS

Tomato-Basil Vinaigrette
5 ripe plum tomatoes, quartered
2 cloves garlic, smashed
½ shallot, sliced
½ cup sherry vinegar, divided
¼ cup sugar
2 cups extra-virgin olive oil, divided
6 basil leaves
Salt and pepper

Crab Salad
2 cups jumbo lump crabmeat
¼ cup mango, peeled, small dice
1 tablespoon chives, finely chopped
¼ cup Tomato Basil Vinaigrette
Salt and pepper

Seafood Tasting:
Tuna Tartare with Soy-Sesame Vinaigrette Serves Eight

INGREDIENTS

Soy-Sesame Vinaigrette
2 tablespoons rice wine vinegar
¾ cup sesame oil
½ cup soy sauce
Salt and pepper

Tuna Tartare
2 cups sushi-grade tuna,
   small dice
1 tablespoon black
   sesame seeds
¼ cup avocado,
   peeled and small dice
2 tablespoons
   Soy-Sesame Vinaigrette
¼ cup scallions, thinly sliced on
   the bias

Note: This recipe is part of the Seafood Tasting set of recipes, which serves eight.

SOY-SESAME VINAIGRETTE
Whisk all the ingredients together in a bowl. Season with salt and pepper. Reserve.

TUNA TARTARE
Combine the tuna, sesame seeds and vinaigrette in a medium-sized bowl. Gently fold in the avocado. Garnish each portion with a few scallion slices.

Seafood Tasting:
Scallop Ceviche with Hazelnut Vinaigrette Serves Eight

INGREDIENTS

Hazelnut Vinaigrette
¼ cup hazelnut oil
¼ cup red wine vinegar
¼ cup extra-virgin olive oil
Salt and pepper

Scallop Ceviche
5 large scallops, tough muscle
   removed, small dice
½ cup hazelnuts, halved
3 tablespoons Hazelnut
   Vinaigrette
¼ cup microgreens
Coarse sea salt

Note: This recipe is part of the Seafood Tasting set of recipes, which serves eight.

HAZELNUT VINAIGRETTE
Whisk all the ingredients together in a bowl. Season with salt and pepper. Reserve.

SCALLOP CEVICHE
Preheat the oven to 325 degrees. Lay the hazelnuts on a sheet pan and roast for 8–10 minutes. Remove them from the oven and allow to cool. Coarsely chop the nuts and set aside.

Mix the vinaigrette with the diced scallops, and marinate in the refrigerator for 5 minutes. Add the hazelnuts. Adjust the seasoning with coarse sea salt. Garnish each salad with microgreens.

ASSEMBLY
For optimum freshness, assemble all the salads as close to service as possible. On a chilled rectangular plate, spoon ¼ cup of each salad approximately 1 inch apart. Garnish as specified above and serve.

Thin Sliced Tuna with Cashew Dressing Serves Eight

INGREDIENTS

Spice Mixture
1 tablespoon white pepper
1½ tablespoons coriander seed
1½ tablespoons whole
  cumin seed
10 green cardamom pods
¼ teaspoon chili powder
1½ tablespoons ground ginger
1½ tablespoons lemongrass
  powder

Cashew Dressing
¾ cup unsalted cashews, toasted
¼ cup coconut milk
½ teaspoon red curry paste
½ tablespoon sesame oil
¼ cup soy sauce
2 tablespoons sweet chili sauce
  (for Asian spring rolls)
¼ cup rice wine vinegar
¾ cup grapeseed oil
Salt and pepper

Tuna
1 16-ounce block of
  sushi-grade tuna
1 tablespoon grapeseed oil
2 cups black radish, julienne
2 cups daikon radish, julienne
2 cups cello radish, julienne
2 cups haricot verts, blanched,
  shocked and small dice
1 tablespoon cilantro, chiffonade
1 cup cashews, chopped
½ cup scallions, sliced
  (for garnish)
Salt and pepper

SPICE MIXTURE
Combine all the spices and lightly toast them in a hot, dry sauté pan. Allow them to cool, then grind in a coffee grinder.

CASHEW DRESSING
Combine all ingredients, except the grapeseed oil, in a blender. Blend on high speed and drizzle in the oil in a slow, steady stream. Adjust seasoning with salt and pepper.

Note: Cashew dressing can be made ahead and refrigerated for up to 3 days.

ASSEMBLY
Note: Use a mandoline to slice the radishes into a uniform julienne. For the cilantro chiffonade, stack the leaves like a deck of cards then cut them into very thin strands. Don't slice the cilantro too early or it will loose its fresh green color.

Season the tuna with salt then roll it into the spice mixture. Heat a sauté pan on high heat and add the grapeseed oil. When oil is nearly smoking, sear the tuna on each side for 10 seconds. Remove it from the pan and let it rest. When the fish is cool, wrap it in plastic wrap and put it in the freezer until it's partially frozen, approximately 2 hours.

Remove fish from freezer and unwrap. If the fish has frozen solid, let it stand at room temperature for about 10 minutes. With a sharp knife, cut very thin slices from the narrow end of the tuna. In the restaurant, we use a deli slicer for this. Lay the slices out on a plate or small sheet pan lined with parchment paper and refrigerate until needed.

Note: The tuna can be frozen and sliced a few hours ahead. Just wrap the plate in plastic and refrigerate.

Toss the radishes, green beans, haricot verts, cashews and cilantro with ½ cup of the dressing. Adjust the seasoning with salt and pepper. Pile 1 cup of the salad high on a plate. Shingle the tuna slices atop the salad, slightly overlapping each piece. Garnish with sliced scallions and additional dressing, if desired.

NOTES
SPECIAL EQUIPMENT: Electric coffee/spice grinder, mandoline.

 WINE PAIRING: The combination of the spice rub and the cashew dressing calls for a wine that is crisp and fruity. Try a light German Riesling with just a touch of sweetness.

Venison Carpaccio Serves Eight

In a spice grinder, grind the cardamom, fennel seeds, black pepper, star anise, cloves and grains of paradise into a powder. Transfer the mix to a bowl and fold in the cinnamon and salt.

Dry the venison loin with a clean kitchen towel. Liberally sprinkle the spice mixture over the entire loin and rub the spices in with your hand.

Heat a large sauté pan on high heat. When the pan is hot, add the grapeseed oil. Sear the venison loin for approximately 10 seconds on each side. Place the venison on a sheet tray and let it cool to room temperature, about 20 minutes.

Place the loin horizontally on a piece of plastic wrap about 2 feet long. Roll the venison tightly in the plastic like a piece of candy. The purpose is to compact the venison into a tight cylinder. Wrap the venison with another piece of plastic so the seal doesn't unravel and freeze it until solid.

When the venison is frozen, remove the plastic. The setting on your meat slicer should be very thin, between 0 and 1 on most slicers. Holding the venison with a kitchen towel, position the loin perpendicular to the blade. Carefully slice the loin and lay the slices in a circular pattern on 8 serving plates. Wrap each plate tightly in plastic until ready to serve.

ASSEMBLY

Sprinkle the sliced venison with sea salt and drizzle with olive oil. Toss the jicama with ½ tablespoon of olive oil, lemon juice, chives and salt. Place approximately ¼ cup of the dressed jicama directly in the center of each plate. Complete the dish with the arugula, figs, pine nuts and Parmesan. Serve immediately.

NOTES

SPECIAL EQUIPMENT: Electric meat slicer.

 WINE PAIRING: This venison dish is a great cold starter that works well in the fall and early winter. Try pairing it with an American Chardonnay, perhaps from Napa Valley. Choose a wine that has creamy notes with just a hint of oak.

INGREDIENTS

½ cup grains of paradise
2 whole cloves
½ teaspoon ground cinnamon
2½ whole star anise
2 tablespoons green
   cardamom pods
2 tablespoons fennel seeds
2 tablespoons black peppercorns
2 tablespoons salt
1 venison short loin, cleaned of
   all sinew and silver skin
2 tablespoons grapeseed oil

Garnish

1 cup dried figs, quartered
1 cup pine nuts, lightly toasted
2 cups jicama, julienne
1 cup micro arugula
1½ tablespoons chives, finely
   chopped
½ tablespoon lemon juice
1 cup Parmesan cheese, shaved
Extra-virgin olive oil
Coarse sea salt

Watermelon Sashimi Serves Eight

Like many recipes, Watermelon Sashimi was conceived somewhat by accident. One evening, the staff and I were eating watermelon with our pre-service dinner. We had some melon left over, so we Cryovac'ed it. The next day, I noticed the watermelon had intensified in color. It looked like a block of sushi-grade tuna. When I tasted it, the flavor had intensified as well. The vacuum forced all the melon's juice to the center, concentrating its sweetness. I thought a dish playing off the sashimi concept would be fun and great for summer. However, the first few attempts used an array of Asian ingredients and misfired with disastrous and nearly inedible results. Perhaps I had overthought the concept. It was still watermelon, after all. Simply combining it with ingredients you might find at a summer picnic—grapes, crumbled feta and sunflower seeds—proved most delicious.

INGREDIENTS

1 large seedless watermelon

½ cup sunflower seeds

1 cup feta cheese, crumbled

24 red grapes, quartered

4 tablespoons extra-virgin
   olive oil

1 cup microgreens (arugula,
   spinach, mizuna, etc.)

Coarse sea salt and cracked
   black pepper

Using a serrated knife, peel the watermelon by first cutting the rind off the narrow top and bottom. With the watermelon on its end, cut away the rind in several vertical strips. When the watermelon is completely peeled, cut it into thirds.

Individually vacuum seal each piece in a plastic bag using the machine's highest setting. If the watermelon is not fully ripe, you may need to add 1 or 2 tablespoons of simple syrup (1:1 ratio of water and sugar) for additional sweetness. Refrigerate sealed watermelon pieces for 30 minutes.

Remove the watermelon from the bags. Cut the pieces into rectangles approximately 2 inches in width and height. Slice ¼-inch pieces off the blocks.

Lay 6–8 pieces of watermelon horizontally on a plate. Garnish with the sunflower seeds, grapes and feta. Drizzle about a ½ teaspoon of olive oil on and around the "sashimi." Finish with black pepper, sea salt and microgreens.

NOTES

SPECIAL EQUIPMENT: Cryovac or other vacuum-sealing machine.

 WINE PAIRING: The flavors of this dish are clean and sharp, so you need a wine that mimics that. Choose a crisp Chardonnay, one with no oak. The Macon region of Burgundy produces well-priced, vibrant Chardonnay, most without any oakiness. Try a Pouilly-Fuissé or a Saint Véran.

Watermelon Sashimi continues to be a popular summer mainstay at Restaurant Nicholas.

White Almond Gazpacho <small>Serves Eight</small>

Preheat the oven to 325 degrees. Place almonds and bread on separate cookie sheets and lightly toast, about 8 minutes. Remove from the oven and let cool.

Working in three separate batches, puree nuts, bread, garlic, olive oil, sugar, vinegar, salt, pepper and water in blender. Pass the soup through a chinois until a smooth, velvety texture is reached. Chill soup in refrigerator, if necessary.

To serve, ladle the soup in bowls and top with your choice of garnish.

NOTES
SPECIAL EQUIPMENT: Chinois or fine-mesh strainer.

 WINE PAIRING: Keep with the Spanish theme and pair this dish with a crisp, dry white wine from Spain. Wines made with the Albarino grape, which characteristically has racy acidity, are bold enough to stand up to these strong Mediterranean flavors.

INGREDIENTS

8 cups French bread, crusts removed and cut into 1-inch cubes

2 cups white almonds

2½ quarts ice-cold water

1 teaspoon sugar

¼ cup extra-virgin olive oil

¾ cup champagne vinegar

3 cloves Garlic Confit (see page 229)

Salt and white pepper

Optional: Thinly sliced roasted red peppers, sliced grapes, sliced cucumbers, grilled calamari rings, and/or pickled oysters for garnish

Heirloom Tomato Salad with Watermelon Water _Serves Eight_

INGREDIENTS

Basil Oil
3 bunches basil
2 cups grapeseed oil

Balsamic Reduction
1 cup high-quality balsamic
   vinegar

Tomato Salad
¼ large watermelon, rind
   removed
4–5 assorted ripe heirloom
   tomatoes or local seasonal
   tomatoes
1 cup assorted grapes, halved
Coarse sea salt

BASIL OIL

Bring a large pot of salted water to a boil. Pick the basil leaves from their stems. Blanch the basil for 30 seconds then immediately transfer it to an ice bath. Remove the basil from the ice water and dry thoroughly with paper towels. Reserve the ice bath.

Combine the basil and oil in a blender. Puree on the highest setting until the mixture begins to get hot, about 2 minutes. Transfer the basil oil to a metal bowl and cool it down quickly by placing the bowl in ice water. Refrigerate the oil overnight.

The next day, line a fine-mesh strainer with a coffee filter and place it over a plastic container. You can also seal the coffee filter around the perimeter of the plastic container with a rubber band if you don't own a small strainer. Pour the basil oil into the strainer and allow it to filter in the refrigerator for 24 hours. Do not press on or wring out the coffee filter when finished. Just use the pure green oil that has accumulated in the container. Refrigerate the oil for up to 3 days or freeze up to 6 months.

BALSAMIC REDUCTION

Heat the vinegar in a small heavy-bottomed saucepot until it starts to gently bubble. Simmer on low for approximately 10 minutes. The vinegar should become slightly syrupy. The reduction will thicken as it cools. Remove from the heat and cool at room temperature. Transfer the reduced vinegar to a squeeze bottle and refrigerate.

ASSEMBLY

Cut the watermelon into small pieces and juice using the electric juicer. Strain the juice through a chinois or fine-mesh strainer. The sweetness of the watermelon can be adjusted with a touch of sugar.

Slice the tomatoes into wedges and toss them with the grapes, a few drizzles of the basil oil and salt. Make a ring around the perimeter of a serving bowl with the Balsamic Reduction. Pile a few tomatoes in the center of the ring. Pour desired amount of watermelon water into the bowl.

NOTES
SPECIAL EQUIPMENT: Electric fruit/vegetable juicer, plastic squeeze bottles, chinois or fine-mesh strainer.

 WINE PAIRING: An Austrian Grüner Veltliner's very distinct mineral qualities will synchronize nicely with the acidity of the tomatoes.

This is a quick summer salad that can easily be made at home. Because there aren't many ingredients to the dish, it's imperative that the tomatoes are ripe and of the highest quality. Otherwise, don't bother. The grapes are also essential. Paired with the watermelon, they add a sweet punch that nicely plays off the tartness of the tomatoes.

Minted Pea Soup Serves Eight

SOUP STOCK

Combine the first 4 ingredients with the water in a heavy-bottomed pot and simmer until the shallots and garlic are tender, approximately 10 minutes.

SOUP

In order to keep the soup's bright green color, it should be cooked in 2 separate batches. Bring half of the stock to a boil. Blanch half of the peas, spinach and mint for approximately 2 minutes. Puree the mixture until smooth, then pass through a chinois into a bowl that sits on top of a larger bowl of ice. Stir the soup until completely chilled. Repeat with the remaining ingredients.

Ladle the soup into serving bowls and garnish with shaved Parmesan and a few drizzles of balsamic vinegar.

NOTES

SPECIAL EQUIPMENT: Chinois or fine-mesh strainer.

 WINE PAIRING: The combination of peas and mint smells like a spring day. Select a crisp New Zealand Sauvignon Blanc, which tends to be more aromatic than its French and American counterparts.

INGREDIENTS

2 shallots, thinly sliced

1 clove garlic, thinly sliced

¼ cup salt

¼ cup sugar

2 quarts water

1 pound frozen peas

4 cups spinach

½ cup mint

Shaved Parmesan, as needed for garnish (optional)

Balsamic vinegar, as needed for garnish (optional)

HOT STARTERS

Seared Dayboat Scallops with Wilted Frisee and Apple-Truffle Vinaigrette Serves Six

Run the apple wedges through a juicer and discard the pulp. Immediately combine the apple juice and egg white in a blender and blend on high speed. With the blender still running, slowly drizzle in the grapeseed oil, followed by the truffle oil. Add the black truffles and pulse briefly to combine. Do not overmix or the vinaigrette will turn gray. Season with salt and pepper.

Note: Apple-Truffle Vinaigrette can be made ahead and refrigerated for up to 3 days.

Note: Granny Smith apples are essential to this recipe. Their tartness stands up to the strong flavor of the truffles. It is also important to have all of your tools and ingredients organized and ready to go. The vinaigrette must be made immediately after the apples are juiced, or the juice will oxidize and turn from bright green to brown. Also, the apples and egg white need to be kept cold, otherwise they may not emulsify with the oils properly and the dressing will break.

ASSEMBLY

Remove the stem from each head of frisee. With a pair of kitchen shears, trim the frisee into bite-size pieces. Wash thoroughly and dry. Reserve until salad is ready to be assembled.

Note: The scallops should either be cooked in 3 separate pans or in batches. If the sauté pan is overcrowded, its temperature will lower and the scallops will steam in their own juices rather than become golden brown and crisp.

Heat 1 tablespoon of grapeseed oil in a sauté pan on medium-high heat. Season the scallops on both sides with salt and pepper. When the oil is very hot, sear 6 scallops. Do not move your scallops around the pan; let them cook in the spot they are in for at least 2 minutes or until the bottoms begin to brown. Add 2 tablespoons of butter and baste the scallops with the hot butter. Turn the scallops over and continue cooking and basting for another 2 minutes. Transfer the scallops from the pan to a few sheets of paper towels and keep warm. Repeat procedure with the remaining scallops.

For the garnish, heat 1 tablespoon of grapeseed oil in a sauté pan on high heat. When the oil just begins to smoke, add the frisee and toss. Season with salt and pepper. Add the apples and continue tossing for another minute or until the frisee is slightly wilted.

Spoon the frisee and apples onto the center of a plate. Garnish the scallops with chives and place them atop the frisee, 3 to a plate. Drizzle the vinaigrette on and around the scallops.

NOTES

SPECIAL EQUIPMENT: Electric fruit/vegetable juicer.

WINE PAIRING: Because the green apple flavors are very pronounced in this dish, select a wine with similar overtones. Pair it with a young, dry German Riesling.

INGREDIENTS

Apple-Truffle Vinaigrette

2 cold Granny Smith apples, cut into wedges, core removed
1 egg white, cold
2 tablespoons truffle oil
¼ cup grapeseed oil
½ teaspoon black truffles, chopped
Salt and pepper

Scallops

2 heads frisee
18 U10 diver scallops, abductor mussels removed
6 tablespoons butter
3 tablespoons grapeseed oil
1 cup Granny Smith apples, peeled and brunoise
2 tablespoons chives, finely chopped
Salt and pepper

Bouillabaisse Serves Eight

INGREDIENTS

Fennel Stock
2 heads fennel, thinly sliced
4 quarts water
1 bay leaf
1 tablespoon black peppercorns

Bouillabaisse Broth
5 live lobsters
2 tablespoons distilled vinegar
1 pound fish bones from white-fleshed
    fish, such as halibut, cod or bass
2 heads fennel, sliced
½ onion, sliced
2 heads garlic, halved
6 plum tomatoes, halved
2 cups white wine
½ tablespoon saffron
⅓ cup tomato paste
½ cup kosher salt
Grapeseed oil
Salt and black pepper

FENNEL STOCK
Combine all the ingredients in a large pot and bring to a boil. Reduce the flame and simmer for 1 hour. Strain and discard the solids.

Note: Fennel stock can be made ahead and refrigerated for up to 3 days.

BOUILLABAISSE BROTH
Fill a large stockpot with water. Add the vinegar and ½ cup salt and bring it to a boil.

Meanwhile, carefully remove the tail and claws from each lobster. You might want to wear rubber gloves to protect your hands from the lobsters' sharp spines. Separate the tails, pincher claws and crusher claws (the larger of the two). Reserve the bodies for the broth.

Submerge the tails in the boiling water and cook for 1½ minutes. Immediately transfer them to a large ice bath to stop the cooking. Repeat the process with the pincher claws (4½ minutes) and crushers (5½ minutes). The lobster parts should stay in the ice bath until cooled completely, up to 10 minutes. The claws and tails will not be fully cooked.

Remove the tails and claws from the water and allow any excess water to drain off. With a heavy chef's knife, split the tails lengthwise and remove each piece of meat from the shell. Rinse under cold water to remove the vein and any roe. Refrigerate the tail meat until needed.

For the claws, first remove the "knuckle," or arm, attached to each claw. Cut the knuckle with kitchen shears to remove the meat. Holding the claw firmly in your hand, detach the small movable part, being careful to also remove the thin piece of cartilage attached. If the cartilage breaks off inside the claw, however, it can still be removed after the meat is out of the shell.

Hold the claw flat on a cutting board and gently tap it with the back of a chef's knife until it cracks. Remove the meat in one piece and rinse off any of the white substance that remains. Repeat the process with the rest of the claws. Refrigerate the claw meat until needed.

For the bodies, remove the large top shell with your hands and set aside. Using a spoon, scrape off the brown fibrous gills. Rinse the bodies under cold running water to remove any guts. With either a heavy chef's knife or a pair of kitchen shears, cut the lobster body and shells into 3- or 4-inch pieces. They do not need to be uniform.

Coat the bottom of a large heavy-bottomed pot with grapeseed oil. Sweat the fennel, onions and garlic on low heat until the vegetables are tender, approximately 10 minutes. Remove from the heat and reserve in the pot.

Heat a large sauté pan over medium heat. Coat the bottom with grapeseed oil. When the oil is hot, add approximately ⅓ of the cleaned and chopped lobster bodies. Season with salt. Sauté the bodies for 10 minutes, stirring periodically. Remove the bodies from the pan and transfer them to the pot containing the fennel, onions and garlic. Repeat with the remaining lobster bodies in 2 more batches.

continues »

The lobster bodies should have left a layer of dark brown fond on the bottom of the sauté pan. With the flame still on medium, coat the bottom of the pan with grapeseed oil and add the tomatoes. Cook for 10 minutes, stirring frequently. Add the tomato paste and cook for an additional 5 minutes. Deglaze the pan with the white wine, scraping up all the fond left on the bottom. Transfer the tomatoes to the pot with the lobster bodies.

Add the fennel stock and the fish bones to the pot. Bring it to a boil, then reduce the heat and simmer for 45 minutes. Adjust the seasoning with salt. Turn off the heat and add the saffron. Let it steep in the broth for no longer than 15 minutes.

Strain the broth first through a colander then through a chinois or fine-mesh strainer. As you're straining, press on the vegetables and bodies with the back of a ladle to extrude as much flavorful liquid as possible. Discard the solids. Blend the broth well with an immersion blender. Pass the broth through the chinois one final time and adjust the seasoning with salt and pepper.

Note: Bouillabaisse Broth can be made ahead and refrigerated for up to 3 days or frozen for up to 3 months.

GRILLED BREAD
Preheat a grill or grill pan on medium-low heat. Toss the bread slices with half of the olive oil in a large bowl. Season with salt and pepper. Grill the bread on each side until toasted and crunchy. Remove from the grill and return to the bowl. Toss the bread with the remaining olive oil. Lay the toast out on a few layers of paper towels to remove any moisture or excess oil.

SAFFRON ROUILLE
Combine the garlic, egg yolks, toasted bread, saffron and ice cubes in a blender and blend on high. Slowly drizzle in the olive oil to create an emulsion. Season with salt and pepper. The consistency should be similar to mayonnaise. If it is too thick, thin it out with a little water.

Pass the rouille through a chinois. Refrigerate until needed.

ASSEMBLY
Place the clams and mussels in separate pots. Add 1 cup of water to each pot. Cover the pots and place over high heat. The clams and mussels are done when they open. Season the shrimp, monkfish and scallops with salt and pepper. Sauté in grapeseed oil. Add the lobster and cook for another 1–2 minutes.

Place 3 clams, 3 mussels, 2 shrimp, 1 scallop and a few pieces of monkfish and lobster in 8 shallow bowls. Garnish with chopped parsley. Ladle hot Bouillabaisse Broth over the fish. Serve the Saffron Rouille and Grilled Bread on the side.

NOTES
SPECIAL EQUIPMENT: Chinois or fine-mesh strainer, immersion blender.

WINE PAIRING: Classically, Bouillabaisse is served with dry Provençal Rosé. Rosé is best-consumed young, so select one with a current vintage.

Grilled Bread
½ baguette, thinly sliced on a bias
1½ cups extra-virgin olive oil
Salt and black pepper

Saffron Rouille
4 cloves Garlic Confit (see page 229)
2 cups Garlic Confit oil
1 tablespoon saffron
3 pieces Grilled Bread
3 egg yolks
1 cup ice cubes
Salt and black pepper

Seafood
16 shrimp, peeled and deveined
24 cherrystone clams, cleaned
24 mussels, cleaned
1½ pounds monkfish, large dice
8 scallops
Reserved lobster meat, chopped
   into large pieces
2 tablespoons parsley, chopped
Salt and black pepper
Grapeseed oil

Braised Pork Belly Serves Eight

Preheat the oven to 325 degrees. Using a sharp knife, portion the pork belly into approximately 5-inch-by-3-inch rectangles. Tie the ends of each portion so they hold their shape when cooking.

Combine the rest of the ingredients in a Dutch oven or large oven-safe pot. A high-sided roasting pan would also work. Bring the liquid to a boil then reduce the heat to a simmer. Add the pork belly portions and simmer for 20 minutes. Cover the pot and transfer it to the oven. Cook for 3 hours.

Remove the pot from the oven and take off the cover. Allow the bellies to cool in the braising liquid for at least 1 hour.

Transfer the bellies to a sheet pan lined with a wire rack. Refrigerate uncovered for at least 5 hours to dry completely. This step is vital. If the bellies are wet, the skin will not get crispy.

Note: The belly can be braised, dried completely, wrapped in plastic and refrigerated for up to 2 days.

PEANUT DRESSING

In a blender, combine the peanut butter, coconut milk, chili sauce and vinegar. You may have to stop the blender and scrape down the sides several times until the liquid and peanut butter are fully incorporated. With the blender running, drizzle in the grapeseed oil. Adjust the seasoning with salt and pepper.

Note: Peanut Dressing can be made ahead and refrigerated for up to 2 days.

GINGERED PLUOTS

Bring a large pot of water to a boil. Submerge the pluots for 20 seconds then immediately transfer them to an ice bath. When they have cooled completely, remove the skins with a paring knife. Cut the pluots in half and remove the pit. Slice the halved pluots into 2 or 3 wedges and place in a bowl.

Combine the Simple Syrup and ginger and bring to a boil. Pour it over the pluots. Allow the pluots to steep in the ginger syrup until the liquid is cool enough to refrigerate, approximately 30–45 minutes. Reserve.

Note: Gingered Pluots can be made ahead and refrigerated for up to 3 days.

ASSEMBLY

Preheat the oven to 400 degrees. Heat a large sauté pan on medium heat. When hot, add the grapeseed oil. It is important to allow the oil to get hot. If not, the pork belly could stick to the pan and possibly rip. Place the bellies, skin-side down, in the hot oil and transfer the pan to the oven. Cook for 8 minutes. Do not overcrowd the pan. Use more than one pan or cook the bellies in batches if necessary.

Remove the bellies from the pan and allow them to rest for 5 minutes.

Toss the cabbage and peanuts with the Peanut Dressing. Adjust the seasoning with salt and pepper. Mix in the cilantro.

Slice the bellies into ½-inch pieces. Spoon about ⅓ cup of the Cabbage Slaw on a plate. Slice the Gingered Pluots very thinly and fan 3 or 4 pieces on top of the slaw. Shingle the sliced pork next to the salad and serve.

NOTES

SPECIAL EQUIPMENT: Butcher's twine, Dutch oven (optional).

 WINE PAIRING: I like to pair this dish with a German Riesling. The fruitiness of a Riesling is a nice foil for the spiciness of the peanut dressing.

INGREDIENTS

1 pound pork belly
1 gallon Chicken Stock
  (see page 227)
3 cups soy sauce
2 Thai chilies
½ bunch scallions
1 cup ginger, sliced
4 heads garlic, halved
1 tablespoon salt

Peanut Dressing

1 cup peanut butter
¼ cup coconut milk
½ cup sweet chili sauce
½ cup rice wine vinegar
½ cup grapeseed oil
Salt and white pepper

Gingered Pluots

4 ripe pluots or plums
2 cups Simple Syrup
  (see page 230)
1 tablespoon ginger, julienne

Cabbage Slaw

3 cups Napa cabbage, thinly
  sliced
⅓ cup peanuts, rough chopped
2 tablespoons Peanut Dressing
1 tablespoon cilantro, chopped
2 tablespoons grapeseed oil
Salt and white pepper

Risotto with Truffles Serves Eight

This dish works well with either black or white truffles. White truffles become available in the late fall, followed by the black variety in the early winter. High-end retailers such as D'Artagnan will carry both types of truffles when available (check Specialty Stores on page 235).

INGREDIENTS

Truffle Foam
¼ cup heavy cream
2 cups skim milk
2 sheets gelatin, 3 x 8 inches
1½ tablespoons truffle oil
1 teaspoon salt

Risotto
1½ quarts Chicken Stock
  (see page 227)
Grapeseed oil
4 shallots, minced
4 cups Carnaroli rice
½ cup white wine
4 ounces butter
1 cup Parmesan cheese, grated
1 tablespoon truffle trim, roughly
  chopped (optional)
Truffle oil
2 ounces truffles
¼ cup chives, finely chopped
Salt and pepper

TRUFFLE FOAM

Place the gelatin sheets in cold water for 3–4 minutes to allow them to soften or "bloom." In a medium saucepan, reduce heavy cream by half. Add skim milk and bring to a boil. Pull pot off the heat, squeeze out any water from gelatin sheets, and add them to the hot milk. Whisk until the gelatin has dissolved. Add truffle oil and salt.

To create foam, the milk must be warm but not too hot. Tilt the pot so you can submerge the head of the immersion blender. Blend on high until a layer of foam is created on top. Gently skim off the foam with a large spoon.

RISOTTO

Bring the stock to a boil then reduce to the lowest simmer. Place a large, heavy-bottomed pot over medium heat. Coat the bottom with grapeseed oil. Sweat the shallots for about 3 minutes or until translucent. Add the rice and saute for 4 minutes, stirring frequently until the rice begins to turn golden. Deglaze the pan with white wine and continue to cook, stirring frequently until almost all of the wine has evaporated.

Ladle in ½ cup of the hot stock and stir. As the rice absorbs the liquid, ladle in more stock, ½ cup at a time. It is important to stir frequently. Cook for about 20 minutes, adding stock as needed until the rice is tender but not mushy.

Stir in the butter, Parmesan cheese, chopped truffles and a few drizzles of white truffle oil. Adjust the seasoning with salt and white pepper.

Spoon approximately ½ cup of the foam into the center of a bowl. Ladle the risotto atop the foam. Shave desired amount of truffles directly over the risotto. Garnish with chopped chives.

NOTES
SPECIAL EQUIPMENT: Immersion blender.

WINE PAIRING: The classic pairing for truffle risotto is Nebbiolo from Barolo or Barbaresco. I can't argue with tradition here.

Your favorite mushroom can be substituted if truffles
are not available.

Roasted Butternut Squash Soup *Serves Six*

Preheat oven to 350 degrees. Cut butternut squash in half lengthwise and remove seeds. Rub the exposed flesh of the squash with grapeseed oil and place a tablespoon of butter in each cavity. Season with salt and pepper. With the cut side up, roast for approximately an hour and a half or until the squash is golden brown and cooked through. Let the squash cool for 30 minutes then scoop out the flesh with a spoon.

While the squash is roasting, make a sachet by wrapping nutmeg, cloves and cinnamon in a coffee filter and tying the top of the pouch with butcher's twine.

In a heavy-bottomed saucepot, melt remaining butter over a medium-low flame. When the butter starts to foam, add the celery root, carrot, onion and shallot. Lightly season the vegetables with salt and pepper. Continue to cook until the vegetables become translucent, about 10 minutes. Deglaze with Simple Syrup and cranberry juice, scraping the bottom of the pot to loosen any brown bits. Add sachet and cook for an additional 2 minutes. Add the squash, Chicken Stock and water, and bring to a boil. Lower heat and simmer for 1 hour.

Discard the sachet. In a blender, puree the soup in batches and pass through a chinois. Be careful when working with hot liquid; do not fill the blender more than halfway. Add the maple syrup and stir. Adjust the seasoning with salt and pepper.

GARNISH

In a small saucepot, melt butter on medium-high heat. When the butter begins to foam, add the butternut squash and cook for 1 minute, stirring often. Add the bacon and cranberries. Season with salt and pepper.

To serve, place a small spoonful of garnish in each bowl. Lightly drizzle lemon oil around garnish (approximately ¼ of a teaspoon) and sprinkle with cinnamon. Ladle 1 cup of soup directly over garnish and serve.

NOTES
SPECIAL EQUIPMENT: Coffee filter, butcher's twine, chinois or fine-mesh strainer.

 WINE PAIRING: For a dish with such complex spice flavors, like clove, cinnamon and nutmeg, I like an aromatic wine with sweetness on the palate. A German Kabinett Riesling with a little bit of bottle age is a superb match.

INGREDIENTS

1 butternut squash (about 4 pounds)

⅓ cup celery root, peeled and diced

½ cup onion, diced

1 shallot, chopped

¼ cup carrot, diced

1½ quarts Chicken Stock (see page 227)

1 quart water

1 cup cranberry juice

½ cup Simple Syrup (see page 230)

5 tablespoons butter, divided

½ cup maple syrup

1 tablespoon grapeseed oil

1 whole nutmeg, cracked

3 whole cloves

1 stick cinnamon (approximately a 3-inch piece)

For Garnish

½ cup butternut squash, small dice

½ cup bacon lardons (¼-inch strips), cooked

½ cup dried cranberries, rough chopped

½ teaspoon butter

Ground cinnamon

Lemon oil

Roasted Chestnut Soup Serves Six

INGREDIENTS

4 cups raw chestnuts in shell

⅓ cup carrot, medium dice

1 shallot, chopped

1 clove garlic, chopped

½ cup onion, medium dice

3 tablespoons grapeseed oil, divided

2 tablespoons salt

¼ cup brandy

2½ quarts water

¼ cup butter plus 3 teaspoons, divided

½ cup pears, peeled and small dice

½ cup parsnips, peeled and small dice

Preheat oven to 450 degrees. With a paring knife, score a deep cross on the round side of each chestnut. Place scored nuts on a cookie sheet and bake for 20–30 minutes. When done, carefully and quickly remove the shells while the nuts are still warm. The shelling process will be more difficult if the nuts are allowed to cool. Finely dice ½ cup of the chestnuts and reserve for garnish.

Heat 2 tablespoons grapeseed oil in a large saucepan over a medium-high flame, and cook the carrots and onions until they start to brown lightly, about 5–6 minutes. Add chestnuts, garlic, shallots and butter. Cook for another 10–12 minutes, stirring occasionally. When the vegetables and chestnuts are dark brown and caramelized, remove pot from flame and deglaze with brandy, scraping up all the brown bits left on the bottom of the pan. Return the pot to the flame and add the water and salt. Bring to a boil then simmer for 1 hour.

While soup is cooking, prepare the garnish. Blanch parsnips in boiling salted water until tender but not soft, about 1 minute. Strain and shock in ice water. When cool, remove parsnips from water and set aside. In a very hot pan, sauté reserved chopped chestnuts in 1 teaspoon grapeseed oil until they begin to caramelize. Season with salt and finish with 1 teaspoon butter. Remove from pan and reserve. Wipe out pan and individually repeat procedure with parsnips and pears. Add a little sugar to the pears while in the pan if they are underripe. Combine pears, parsnips and chestnuts.

When soup is finished, puree it in a blender (this should be done in 3 or 4 batches) and pass through a chinois. Adjust seasoning if necessary. When blending hot liquid it is important not to fill the blender more than halfway; as the liquid purees the volume will increase.

To serve, spoon a desired amount of garnish in a soup bowl and ladle approximately 1 cup of hot soup over the top.

NOTES

SPECIAL EQUIPMENT: Chinois or fine-mesh strainer.

 WINE PAIRING: This wintertime favorite is best with an earthy Pinot Noir. Gevrey Chambertin from Burgundy's Côte de Nuits is a terrific locale for these complex and food friendly wines.

This soup is best in the summer, when the local corn season is at its peak.

Roasted Corn Soup Serves Eight

Lobster can be omitted from this recipe without losing the fundamental essence of the dish. It's a bit of luxury we like to add at the restaurant. Keep in mind that the more charred the corn is, the smokier the finished product will become. You need to balance that smoke with sweetness. It is also important to use yellow corn since it contains more starch than the white variety.

Remove the kernels from the cobs and reserve. Cut the cobs into thirds. Set a large pot over medium-low heat and coat the bottom with grapeseed oil. Sweat the cobs, onions, garlic and leeks until the vegetables are tender, about 8 minutes. Add the thyme, chili and liquid and bring to a boil. Lower the heat and simmer for 30 minutes. Strain the stock and discard the solids.

Heat a large cast-iron pan on high heat. When the pan is hot, coat the bottom with grapeseed oil and add the corn. You may have to do this in batches. Season the corn with salt and pepper and cook it until the kernels are slightly charred and have a smoky flavor. Be careful, the corn can sometimes pop out of the pan. Reserve ½ cup of corn for the garnish. The corn can also be grilled; keep in mind you are looking for the kernels to be slightly charred.

Puree the kernels with the corn stock and strain through a chinois. This may also be done in batches. Adjust the sweetness of the soup with the maple syrup. Season with salt and pepper.

ASSEMBLY

Bring a small pot of salted water to a boil and add the diced leeks. Cook for about 1 minute or until tender.

Thoroughly wash and dry the chanterelles. Saute them in 1 tablespoon of butter on medium heat until all of the water has cooked out. Season with salt and pepper. Add the corn, leeks, lobster and the other tablespoon of butter. Cook gently until just warmed through.

Spoon a small amount of garnish in the center of a soup bowl. Arrange 3 tomato halves around the corn garnish and lightly drizzle Thyme Oil over them. Ladle the hot soup into each bowl and serve.

NOTES
SPECIAL EQUIPMENT: Chinois or fine-mesh strainer.

WINE PAIRING: A buttery California Chardonnay can have hints of sweet corn that will complement this soup.

INGREDIENTS

8 ears of corn
½ cup leeks, white and pale green parts only, sliced
1 onion, sliced
3 cloves garlic, sliced
3 sprigs thyme, picked
½ Thai chili
2 quarts Chicken Stock (see page 227) or water
Grapeseed oil
⅓ cup maple syrup
Salt and black pepper

Garnish

½ cup cooked lobster meat, rough chopped
½ cup reserved charred corn
¼ cup leeks, white and pale green parts only, small dice
½ cup chanterelle mushrooms
12–15 grape tomatoes, halved
Thyme Oil (see page 231)
1 tablespoon chives, finely chopped
2 tablespoon butter, divided
Salt

Soft-Shell Crab with
Apple-Jicama Slaw and Basil-Citrus Vinaigrette Serves Eight

The soft-shell crab is our most popular first course. Each year, like clockwork, it reappears on our menu the first Tuesday after Mother's Day and remains there throughout the summer. The salad and the vinaigrette are a rendition of a summertime staff meal one of my cooks created. The version you see today is much more refined, but the gist is still there: green apple, jicima, red pepper and citrus basil vinaigrette—all fresh and bright flavors.

INGREDIENTS

Basil-Citrus Vinaigrette
2 cups orange juice
1 shallot, chopped
½ clove garlic, chopped
½ bunch basil leaves
2 cups extra-virgin olive oil, chilled
½ cup ice cubes
1 tablespoon salt
1½ tablespoons sugar

Apple-Jicama Slaw
1 cup Granny Smith apples, julienne
1 cup jicama, peeled and julienne
½ cup red bell pepper, julienne
2 tablespoons cilantro, chiffonade
1 tablespoon lemon juice
3 tablespoon extra-virgin olive oil
Salt and pepper

Soft-Shell Crabs
8 soft-shell crabs
2 cups milk
1 cup farina or Cream of Wheat cereal
Salt
Canola oil, as needed for deep frying

BASIL-CITRUS VINAIGRETTE
In a medium pot, combine the orange juice, shallots and garlic. Reduce over low heat until about ¾ cup remains. Cool immediately in an ice bath. Reserve.

Combine the ice, salt, sugar, ½ cup of orange juice reduction and basil in a blender. Blend on high speed while slowly drizzling in the olive oil. Adjust seasoning if needed. Refrigerate until ready to use.

Note: This vinaigrette must be made the day it is to be used. After a few hours, the flavors go flat and the bright green color dulls.

APPLE-JICAMA SLAW
Toss all ingredients together in a bowl. Season with salt and pepper. This should be done right before serving to prevent the apple from oxidizing.

Note: At the restaurant, we use a Japanese mandoline to make uniform cuts for any salad that calls for julienne fruits or vegetables.

ASSEMBLY
Preheat your deep fryer to 350 degrees or heat oil to temperature in a large heavy-bottomed pot. Check the temperature with a deep-fry thermometer.

In a food processor or blender, process the farina into a fine powder.

With a pair of kitchen shears, remove approximately ½ inch behind the eyes and mouth of the crab. Squeeze out the insides of the sack inside the cut area. Turn the crab over and remove the gills and the small, elongated apron. Rinse each cleaned crab under cold water. Soak the crabs in milk for 15 minutes to help mellow the flavors.

Remove the crabs from the milk and dredge with the farina. Carefully submerge the crab into the oil and cook for 4 minutes. Remove from the oil, season with salt, and let drain on a layer of paper towels.

To serve, spoon ¼ cup of the vinaigrette on the plate. Mound approximately ⅓ cup of the slaw on the top half of the vinaigrette. Lean the crab against the salad.

NOTES
SPECIAL EQUIPMENT: Home deep fryer or deep-fry thermometer.

 WINE PAIRING: The components of this dish are reminiscent of the summer, so try a Pouilly Fumé. Made from Sauvignon Blanc grapes, this wine from the eastern side of France's Loire Valley contains similar summer notes, specifically green apple.

When making the vinaigrette, keep in mind all of the ingredients need to be ice cold, hence the ice cubes. If the ingredients are too warm, you run the risk of the vinaigrette separating in two.

Truffle Egg Custard with Truffle Crème Serves Six

An egg topper is a great tool for creating elegant presentations out of an ordinary egg. It simply makes a clean cut at the egg's narrow end, allowing it to be hollowed out and used as a serving vessel. At the restaurant, we use a sort of "popper" tool, where a lever is pulled like a pinball machine and gently pops the piece out. Although a rare find, they can be found at high-end cooking supply stores such as JB Prince, Sur La Table and Williams-Sonoma, as well as certain Asian markets (see Specialty Stores on page 235).

TRUFFLE CRÈME

Whip the heavy cream in a mixing bowl until soft peaks form. Whisk in salt and truffle oil. Fill a small piping bag fitted with a plain tip with the crème, and refrigerate until needed. Allow crème to come to room temperature before serving.

CUSTARD

With an egg topper, remove the narrow end of each egg. Pour out the inside and reserve. In a deep bowl, soak the eggshells in a mixture of white vinegar and hot tap water for 20 minutes. Remove the shells from the water and very carefully peel off the inner membrane and any pieces of loose shell. Return the shells to the egg carton, cut-side down, to dry.

Construct a double boiler by placing a stainless steel or glass bowl over a pot of boiling water, making sure the water doesn't touch the bottom of the bowl. Add eggs, heavy cream, salt and pepper, and vigorously whisk until the eggs thicken slightly and form ribbons.

Pass the egg mixture through a chinois. Whisk in the truffle oil, chopped truffles, salt and pepper. Transfer to a squeeze bottle and hold in very warm water until ready to use.

ASSEMBLY

Fill 6 espresso cups halfway with rice. Place the shells in the cups and fill ¾ of the shell with the egg custard. Fill the remainder of the shell with Truffle Crème. Garnish with chives and a slice of black truffle. Serve each egg with a spoon small enough to fit inside the eggshell, such as a demitasse spoon used for espresso.

NOTES

SPECIAL EQUIPMENT: Pastry piping bag with a plain tip, egg topper, chinois or fine-mesh strainer, squeeze bottle, 6 espresso cups.

 WINE PAIRING: The Truffle Egg Custard makes an elegant first course and pairs perfectly with Champagne. Alternatively, if you plan on serving this dish in the middle of the meal, a Barbera or Barbaresco from Northern Italy complements the black truffle nicely.

INGREDIENTS

Truffle Crème

½ cup heavy cream
⅛ teaspoon salt
⅛ teaspoon truffle oil

Custard

6 eggs (save carton)
½ cup heavy cream
½ teaspoon salt
1 turn cracked white pepper
¼ teaspoon truffle oil
½ teaspoon chopped black
   truffles
2 teaspoons white vinegar
2 quarts very hot tap water

Garnish

6 slices black truffle
2 cups uncooked rice (for holding
   eggs upright when serving)
½ teaspoon chives,
   finely chopped

Stuffed Squash Blossom
with Ratatouille and Roasted Eggplant Serves Eight

Squash blossoms are highly perishable, therefore most supermarkets will not carry them. High-end food retailers such as Whole Foods should be able to special order them. Some outdoor markets will carry them as well. There are winter and summer varieties. At the restaurant, we use the latter.

INGREDIENTS

Roasted Eggplant
3 medium size eggplant (approximately 1 pound each)
¼ cup capers, finely chopped
2 tablespoons parsley, finely
   chopped
4 cloves garlic, finely chopped
1 shallot, finely chopped
½ cup balsamic vinegar
2 tablespoons sherry vinegar
½ cup extra-virgin olive oil
Wondra flour
⅓ cup grapeseed oil
Salt and pepper

Ratatouille
1 cup eggplant, small dice
½ cup zucchini, small dice
½ cup yellow squash, small dice
½ cup red onion, small dice
1 red bell pepper, peeled and
   small dice
1 clove garlic, finely chopped
2 plum tomatoes, concasse and
   small dice
1 teaspoon parsley, chopped
½ teaspoon oregano, chopped
2 tablespoons extra-virgin
   olive oil
Salt and pepper

Arugula Pesto
½ cup pine nuts
½ clove garlic, rough chopped
¼ cup Parmesan, grated
⅓ cup water
¾ cup extra-virgin olive oil
10 cups arugula
Salt and pepper

ROASTED EGGPLANT
Preheat oven to 325 degrees. Cut the eggplant into 1½-inch rounds. Liberally season each piece on both sides with salt then dust both sides with Wondra.

Heat a large skillet on medium-high heat. When the pan is hot, add the grapeseed oil. Working in batches so as not to crowd the pan, cook the eggplant for approximately 2–3 minutes on each side. The flesh should be a dark roasted brown color. Transfer the eggplant to a roasting pan and roast for 35 minutes.

Remove the eggplant from the oven and lower the temperature to 275 degrees. Transfer the eggplant into a new roasting pan. Drizzle the balsamic vinegar, sherry vinegar and olive oil over the eggplant slices.

Mix the capers, garlic, shallot and parsley in a bowl. Spoon the mixture over the eggplant. Roast in the oven for an additional 25 minutes at 275 degrees. Remove and let cool in the refrigerator.

Cut the eggplant into large cubes. Adjust the seasoning with salt and pepper.

RATATOUILLE
Heat a large sauté pan on medium-high heat. When hot, add the extra-virgin olive oil. Start by adding the onions, then add the garlic, eggplant, red pepper, zucchini, yellow squash and tomatoes. Stir frequently. Cook the vegetables for approximately 8 minutes or until they are cooked through. Remove from the heat and add the herbs. Adjust the seasoning with salt and pepper.

ARUGULA PESTO
Toast the pine nuts in a dry, medium-sized sauté pan on low heat until slightly browned, about 4 minutes. Transfer them to a blender along with the Parmesan, garlic and water. Blend on high for 1 minute. Add the arugula and olive oil, and blend for another minute. Season with salt and pepper. Refrigerate until needed.

TEMPURA
Mix all of the dry ingredients together. Whisk in the club soda a little at a time until the consistency of a loose pancake batter is reached. All of the club soda may not be needed.

continues »

This dish in its entirety can be fairly challenging. However, each component can stand on its own in other applications. The pesto can be used as a sauce for a pasta dish or a spread for a sandwich. The Roasted Eggplant and Ratatouille are both wonderful sides for chicken or meat dishes.

ASSEMBLY

Preheat the oven to 400 degrees. Preheat the oil in the deep fryer to 325 degrees. If you are using a pot on the stovetop, bring the oil up to 325 degrees over a medium flame. You may have to adjust the flame until the temperature holds at around 325.

Place the Ratatouille in the pastry bag. Carefully fill each blossom with 2–3 tablespoons of the Ratatouille and gently twist the tip to seal it. Holding the stem, dip one of the blossoms in the Tempura batter and shake off some of the excess. Fry each blossom for 2 minutes. Do this in small batches to avoid overcrowding. As the blossoms finish cooking, transfer them to a sheet pan lined with a few layers of paper towels. Season with salt and keep warm until all the blossoms are done.

Spoon ½ cup of the eggplant into the centers of 8 large bowls. Carefully spoon ¼ cup of the Arugula Pesto around the eggplant. You can also use a squeeze bottle for this. Place 2 Tempura Squash Blossoms on the eggplant and serve.

NOTES

SPECIAL EQUIPMENT: Pastry bag with a plain tip, home deep fryer (optional), deep-fry thermometer (optional).

 WINE PAIRING: When the flavors of a dish are truly complex, sometimes the best pairing is a simple wine. A dry fruity Rosé is refreshing with these strong Mediterranean flavors.

Tempura

1 cup cake flour

¼ cup cornstarch

½ tablespoon salt

½ tablespoon plus ½ teaspoon baking powder

1½ cups club soda, cold

Squash Blossoms

16 squash blossoms, 2 inches of stem attached

2 quarts canola oil (for deep frying)

Steamed Spaghetti Squash
with Tomato Stew and Arugula Pesto Serves Eight

SPAGHETTI SQUASH

Preheat the oven to 400 degrees. Halve the spaghetti squash lengthwise. Remove the seeds and the fibrous strands. Brush the flesh with extra-virgin olive oil. Season with salt and pepper. Fill a baking pan with 1 inch of water and place the squash halves in it, skin-side up. Cover the pan with foil and bake for 30 minutes.

Remove the squash from the oven and allow it to cool at room temperature. When the squash is cool enough to handle, run a fork lengthwise along the interior. The flesh will release into spaghetti-like strands. Refrigerate the strands until needed.

TOMATO STEW

Preheat the oven to 300 degrees. Toss the tomatoes, garlic, shallot, thyme and oregano with olive oil. Season with salt. Transfer the mixture to a baking pan. The tomato halves should be skin-side down. Roast for 45 minutes.

Remove the tomato mixture from the oven and let it cool at room temperature for 10 minutes. Peel the skin from each tomato and discard. Transfer the mixture to a blender and puree until smooth.

Heat a heavy-bottomed saucepot on medium-low heat. When the pan is hot, add the grapeseed oil. Sweat the carrots for 4 minutes, stirring periodically. Add the onions and celery and cook for an additional 5 minutes. Add the leeks and cook for 2 more minutes. When all the vegetables are soft, deglaze the pan with white wine. Reduce the wine until the pan is almost dry. Add the vegetable stock and reduce it by half.

Add the tomato puree. Raise the heat to high and bring it to a boil. Reduce the heat and simmer for 8–10 minutes or until it has thickened, stirring frequently to prevent the stew from sticking to the bottom. Adjust the seasoning with salt and set aside.

ARUGULA PESTO

Puree all the ingredients in a blender until smooth. Season with salt and pepper. Transfer the pesto to a squeeze bottle and refrigerate until needed.

ASSEMBLY

Place the spaghetti squash, butter and water in a heavy-bottomed pot. Gently warm through on low heat. Adjust the seasoning with salt. In another pot, heat up the tomato stew.

Place a 3-inch ring mold in the center of a shallow bowl. Fill the mold with the squash. Gently remove the mold. Spoon the stew around the squash. Squeeze the pesto around the exterior of the stew. Garnish with the arugula leaves, toasted pine nuts and shaved Parmesan.

NOTES

SPECIAL EQUIPMENT: 3-inch ring mold, squeeze bottle.

WINE PAIRING: This dish demands a rich wine but not an oaky one. I love to pair Viognier with it. The wine is full bodied and creamy yet has no trace of oak.

INGREDIENTS

Spaghetti Squash

1 medium-sized spaghetti squash
Extra-virgin olive oil
Salt and black pepper

Tomato Stew

5 ripe plum tomatoes, halved
  lengthwise
1 shallot, rough chopped
2 cloves garlic, rough chopped
4–5 oregano leaves
3 sprigs thyme, picked
1 cup carrot, medium dice
1 cup onion, medium dice
1 cup celery, medium dice
1 cup leeks, medium dice
¼ cup extra-virgin olive oil
3 tablespoons grapeseed oil
½ cup white wine
½ cup Vegetable Stock
  (see page 231)

Arugula Pesto

1 cup baby arugula
½ clove garlic
2 tablespoons pine nuts, toasted
2 tablespoons Parmesan cheese,
  grated
½ cup extra-virgin olive oil
Salt and pepper

Garnish

½ cup pine nuts, toasted
1 cup baby arugula
½ cup Parmesan cheese, shaved
2 tablespoons butter
¼ cup water
Salt

Cavatelli with Garlic Emulsion and Spring Vegetables Serves Four

INGREDIENTS

Cavatelli
¾ cup durum flour, plus more for dusting
¼ cup warm water

Spring Onions
5 spring onions
½ cup extra-virgin olive oil
¼ cup white wine vinegar
1 teaspoon sugar
1 tablespoon grapeseed oil
Salt

English Peas
1 cup shucked English peas
1 cup pea shoots

Garlic Butter Emulsion
½ pound butter, cubed
½ cup Roasted Garlic Stock (see page 230)
¼ cup extra-virgin olive oil
Salt and pepper

CAVATELLI
Mound the flour in a large bowl and create a well in the center. Pour the water directly into the well. Slowly incorporate the flour into the water with your fingers. The dough should be slightly crumbly. Work the dough into one solid piece. Set your pasta machine on its highest setting and run the dough through 3 or 4 times, rotating the dough with each pass. Lower the dial until the pasta is approximately ¼ inch thick.

With a sharp knife, trim the dough into a rectangle. Portion the dough into ¾-inch strips, then cut the strips into ½-inch rectangles. Lightly dust the pasta pieces with durum flour.

To shape the cavatelli, place a piece of dough horizontally in front of you. Press down on the dough with your index and middle fingers while slightly pushing forward. Then roll the piece gently backward to form a concave shape. The pasta can be frozen in freezer bags until ready to use.

SPRING ONIONS
These onions are cooked "sous vide." Bring a large pot of water to 190 degrees. At this temperature, bubbles will form on the bottom of the pot but will not break the surface. Maintain the temperature with a thermometer. If the water exceeds 190 degrees, the vacuum seal on the bag may break.

Remove the green stalks and stems from the onions. Place the bulbs in a vacuum bag with the olive oil, vinegar, sugar and salt. Seal the bag and submerge it in the water for 20 minutes. If the bag floats, you may need to weigh it down with an ovenproof plate. Remove the onions from the water and let them cool for 10 minutes inside the bag. Open the bag and slice the onions in half lengthwise.

Heat the grapeseed oil in a sauté pan on medium-high heat. Place the onions cut-side down and cook until caramelized. Transfer them to a paper towel to cool, then slice them lengthwise again into quarters.

Note: If you're not sous-vide savvy, this can easily be done on the stovetop with good results. Clean the spring onions the same way. Place them in a sauté pan with the salt, sugar, white wine vinegar and olive oil. Heat the liquid until it just begins to boil, then reduce the flame to its lowest setting and cover. Cook for 10 minutes. To check for doneness, pierce one of the onions with a paring knife. If the knife penetrates with little resistance, the onions are done. Transfer the onions to a few layers of paper towels to drain. Slice the onions in half lengthwise, then follow the above procedure for caramelizing them.

ENGLISH PEAS
Cook the peas for 1½ minutes in a large pot of boiling, salted water. Drain and transfer them to an ice bath. When the peas are completely cool, reserve them in a bowl lined with a few paper towels to absorb any excess water. Cut the pea shoots in half if they are large. Reserve.

GARLIC BUTTER EMULSION
Bring the Roasted Garlic Stock to a simmer in a medium-size saucepan. Whisk in the butter, piece by piece. When the butter has melted, slowly drizzle in the olive oil while whisking vigorously to suspend it with the butter. Season with salt and pepper.

ASSEMBLY
Drop the cavatelli into a large pot of boiling, salted water. Cook for 4 minutes. Meanwhile, heat the onions and peas in a little grapeseed oil and season with salt. Add the pea shoots to the onions and peas just to wilt. Add 1 tablespoon of Garlic Butter Emulsion to the vegetables. Stir in the cooked cavatelli.

Serve approximately 20–22 pieces of cavatelli per person, along with the vegetables. Garnish each plate with a fried basil leaf, if desired.

NOTES
SPECIAL EQUIPMENT: Pasta machine, Cryovac or other vacuum-sealing machine, instant-read thermometer.

 WINE PAIRING: This dish needs a wine with great acidity. A Sancerre or Muscadet from the Loire Valley will have the requisite acidity to cut through the buttery richness of the olive oil sauce.

Making the cavatelli can be somewhat of a challenge, but if you have the time, equipment and patience, I recommend trying it. The final product is very light and elegant. Your guests will go crazy. However, a quality store-bought cavatelli would also work.

The version we had in France was accompanied with a truffle-and-leek sauce. Our version uses sugar snap peas and artichokes. This gnocchi will work with a variety of vegetables, so substitute your favorites. Use the Carrot Stock recipe (page 227) as the base of your butter sauce if you prepare this dish without artichokes.

Gnocchi à la Parisienne Serves Eight

Truth be told, I'm no superchef. I don't have religious epiphanies before coming up with recipes. They don't appear in my dreams. Before a dish is put on the menu, it's tested and retested several times. And even after it hits the menu, we'll often tweak and adjust it until finally we have a product that I am comfortable with. Sometimes this takes a few days. Sometimes it takes a few years. The Parisian Gnocchi is an example of the latter.

While traveling through France, Melissa and I tasted a gnocchi dish that was like no other. The gnocchi were light and airy with a crisp exterior—very different from traditional gnocchi. Melissa loved it and suggested I recreate it at the restaurant.

When we returned to New Jersey, I dusted off some old cookbooks in search of the recipe. Batch after batch came up short. "Nope, that's not it either," Melissa would say after tasting what must have been her umpteenth plate of gnocchi. I tried all sorts of recipes, different potatoes, different flours and different cooking methods. Some worked better than others, but nothing was like what we had in France. We were opening the restaurant at the time, so I had a million other things on my mind. As much as I was intent on nailing this recipe, it would have to wait.

Flash forward to the following summer. The restaurant was off the ground and I now had time to play with more gnocchi recipes. My kitchen crew got involved this time and they created some beautiful dishes, unfortunately none of which were what I was looking for.

One year later, I had just about given up on my gnocchi quest when I discovered a recipe void of traditional potatoes. Instead, it was made with pâte à choux, a classic French dough. We tried it out, but it still came up short. This was getting ridiculous. Maybe my wife's memory was foggy? Perhaps it was too long ago? Possibly the gnocchi in France wasn't actually as good as she remembered? It was our honeymoon, after all, so maybe she had associated the dish with a happier time? Like the first time you eat a hotdog at Yankee Stadium, it's the best thing ever. You have that same hotdog someplace else and it's just not as good. Surely that was the case. Frustrated, I decided that there would be no more gnocchi experiments at Restaurant Nicholas.

In the four years that passed I convinced myself that I really didn't even like gnocchi. And it probably wouldn't look right on our menu anyway. It was for the best. Then I accidentally stumbled upon a pâte-à-choux gnocchi recipe in which the dough pieces were poached in 180-degree water rather than cooked in boiling water. "Hey, what the hell," I thought, "I'll try it."

Lo and behold that was it! Turned out that Melissa's memory wasn't skewed after all. And I actually did like gnocchi. After four years and a library's worth of recipes, we had our dish!

The key to this recipe is poaching the dough in 180-degree water. Any hotter and the gnocchi will deflate when you cook them. The crunch comes from the Parmesan cheese added right at the end. If it's made properly, you will be left with airy, crunchy little pillows.

People adore this dish and they often ask where I came up with the recipe. I would love to tell them it was hand delivered by angels, but now you know that's just not the case.

INGREDIENTS

Gnocchi

1 cup milk
2 ounces butter
1 cup all-purpose flour
3 eggs
1 teaspoon salt
1 ounce Parmesan, grated
Pinch of nutmeg
⅓ cup grapeseed oil
2 tablespoons butter
¼ cup grated Parmesan

GNOCCHI

Bring the milk and butter to boil. Add all the flour at once, reduce the heat to medium-low, and cook for 12 minutes, continuously stirring.

Transfer the dough to a stand mixer fitted with the paddle attachment and mix on medium speed. Add the first egg. When it is completely incorporated into the dough, add the second egg. Repeat the process with the third egg. Add the salt, nutmeg and cheese.

Bring a large pot of salted water to 180 degrees, just below boiling. If the water temperature is too high, the gnocchi will fall apart while cooking.

Place the dough in a pastry bag with a small round tip. Working in batches, squeeze out ½-inch pieces of dough and cut them off with a paring knife or kitchen shears directly into the water. Cook for 8–10 minutes. Remove the gnocchi from the water and submerge them in an ice bath just until cool. Transfer them to a lightly oiled sheet pan.

continues »

Baby Artichokes
12–14 baby artichokes
1 carrot, medium dice
1 onion, medium dice
1 shallot, sliced
1 clove garlic
1 tablespoon grapeseed oil
Salt and pepper
3 sprigs thyme
2 quarts Chicken Stock
  (see page 227)
½ cup white wine
10 lemons, juiced

Sugar Snap Peas
8 ounces sugar snap peas

Fried Leeks
1 medium leek, white part only
½ cup grapeseed oil
Salt

Artichoke-Butter Sauce
½ cup reduced artichoke
  braising liquid
8 ounces butter, cubed
Salt and pepper

BABY ARTICHOKES
In a large pot or Dutch oven set on medium-low heat, sweat the carrots, onions, shallot and garlic in the grapeseed oil for 10 minutes or until tender. Season with salt and pepper. Deglaze the pot with white wine and reduce until nearly all the wine has evaporated. Add the Chicken Stock and bring to a boil. Reduce heat to a simmer.

While the broth is simmering, remove the outer leaves from each artichoke and cut off the tops. Trim the sides and stem into a smooth cylinder shape. Submerge each artichoke into the lemon juice to prevent oxidization.

When all of the artichokes have been trimmed, add them to the simmering liquid. Cover and cook on medium heat for 15 minutes. Insert a paring knife into one of the artichokes. If the knife slides through with no resistance, the artichokes are done.

Remove the artichokes and strain the liquid. Quarter the artichokes and store them in 2 cups of the liquid until ready to use. Reduce the remaining liquid by half and reserve.

SUGAR SNAP PEAS
Bring a large pot of salted water to a boil. Add the peas and cook for 1 minute. Shock in an ice bath. Remove the peas from the ice water and drain on paper towels. Cut off and discard the fibrous string running down the seam of each pod. Pull the pods in half and reserve.

FRIED LEEKS
Slice the white part of the leek into 3-inch pieces, then cut the pieces in half lengthwise. Remove and discard the centers and cut the halves into julienne strips. Thoroughly wash in cold water and dry.

In a high-sided sauté pan, heat the oil on medium-high heat. When the oil is hot, add the leeks, stirring frequently until they are slightly brown. Remove from the oil and drain on a towel. Season with salt. Reserve.

ARTICHOKE-BUTTER SAUCE
Bring the reduced artichoke liquid to a boil in a medium saucepot and reduce slightly. Lower the heat and whisk in the butter, one piece at a time. Adjust the seasoning with salt and pepper.

Note: The sauce is quite delicate. It should be made right before serving.

ASSEMBLY
Place the artichokes and snap peas in a medium saucepot along with 2–3 tablespoons of the Artichoke-Butter Sauce. Gently warm through.

Heat a heavy-bottomed sauté pan on medium-high heat. Add ⅓ cup of grapeseed oil. When the oil is hot, add the gnocchi and sauté for 1 minute. Add 2 tablespoons of butter and cook for an additional minute or until the gnocchi are golden brown. Add the Parmesan and cook for 15 seconds, tossing frequently. Remove the gnocchi from the oil and drain in a colander or on paper towels.

Serve the gnocchi in a bowl with the snap peas and artichokes. Spoon 2 tablespoons of Artichoke-Butter Sauce around the gnocchi. Garnish the top with the Fried Leeks.

NOTES
SPECIAL EQUIPMENT: Electric stand mixer with paddle attachment, pastry bag with a round tip.

 WINE PAIRING: The wines of Fruili, in northeastern Italy, are full-bodied and complex. Unique indigenous grape varieties, such as Ribolla Giallo, can be an excellent complement to the artichoke and sharp Parmesan cheese.

Pumpkin Agnolotti Serves Eight

Making the agnolotti is not as difficult as it seems, though it will take some practice to get the technique down. Alternatively, you can make mini-raviolis using the same dough and filling.

INGREDIENTS

Pumpkin Filling
1 small butternut squash
1 small sweet potato
1 15-ounce can pumpkin puree
1 tablespoon honey
2 tablespoons butter
Pinch of freshly grated nutmeg
Pinch of freshly grated cinnamon
Salt and pepper

Pumpkin Agnolotti
Pasta Dough (see page 230)
All-purpose flour,
   as needed for dusting

PUMPKIN FILLING

Preheat the oven to 350 degrees. Cut the butternut squash in half lengthwise and scoop out the seeds with a spoon. Place the halves on a sheet pan lined with a rack, skin-side down. Season with salt and pepper. Place 1 tablespoon of butter in each cavity. Add the sweet potato to the same sheet pan. Roast for 45–60 minutes. Remove the sheet tray from the oven and let the squash and sweet potato cool for 15 minutes.

With a paring knife, peel the skin off the sweet potato. Add the potato to a blender. Spoon out the roasted squash from their shells and combine it with the potato. Puree on the highest setting until smooth.

Pass the puree through a tamis using a rubber spatula. Fold the pumpkin, honey, cinnamon and nutmeg into the squash-potato mixture. Adjust seasoning with salt and pepper. Store in the refrigerator until ready to use.

PUMPKIN AGNOLOTTI

Divide the pasta dough into three separate pieces and cover with plastic wrap. With the heel of your hand, flatten one of the portions to a size that will fit into your pasta machine. On the highest setting, pass the pasta through twice. Lower the setting one notch and pass it through two more times. Fold the two long ends into the center and press down with the heel of your hand, making the dough into a rectangle.

Pass the dough through with the folded crease pointing vertically into the machine. Continue passing the dough through, lowering the dial with each pass, until the pasta is a thin sheet. Position the sheet in front of you horizontally on a floured work surface.

Cut the sheet of dough in half lengthwise so there are 2 long sheets of dough, each about 3 inches wide. If your pasta machine is small, you may not need to do this. Trim the ends of each piece to make them relatively equal in size.

Transfer the pumpkin filling to the piping bag and pipe a long strip directly across the middle of each sheet. Take the bottom half of the sheet and fold it over the filling. With your finger, gently press down on the dough alongside the filling to create a seal.

Starting at one end of each sheet, pinch a pillow about an inch wide by giving a gentle push inward with both hands. Continue until both sheets have small pillows about ¾ inch apart. With a crimped pastry wheel, trim the dough at the top, leaving about a ½-inch lip. Carefully slide a small offset spatula underneath the dough to release it from the work surface. Run the pastry wheel forward between the pillows. The agnolotti will release, one by one.

continues »

This is one of my favorite dishes. All the components
are reminiscent of an autumn harvest.

Place the finished pasta on a floured sheet pan. Continue with the remaining pieces of dough. When finished, place the sheet pan in the refrigerator until ready to use. The pasta can also be frozen and stored in freezer bags for later use.

BROWN BUTTER SAUCE

Melt the Carrot Stock over medium heat. When hot, whisk in the butter cubes, one at a time. Be careful. If the flame is too high or too low, the butter will not emulsify with the liquid, and the sauce will break. After the butter, whisk in the brown butter. Continue whisking until the brown butter is completely emulsified. Season with salt and pepper.

This sauce is fragile. If made too early and left to cool, it will break. It should be made right before serving and kept warm.

ASSEMBLY

Lightly toast the pumpkin seeds in a sauté pan on medium-low heat. Remove the seeds from the pan and reserve. Sauté the squash in butter until lightly browned. Season with salt and pepper and reserve.

Bring a large pot of salted water to a boil. Cook the agnolotti for 4 minutes. Meanwhile, warm up the squash and pumpkin seeds in a large pot with the butter. Add the agnolotti and toss everything with the Brown Butter Sauce. Remove from heat and stir in the sage.

Serve approximately 8 agnolotti per bowl along with the garnish. Top with the grated truffled cheese.

NOTES

SPECIAL EQUIPMENT: Fine-mesh tamis, pasta machine, piping bag with a plain ½-inch tip, crimped pastry wheel, small offset spatula.

 WINE PAIRING: The country wine of Alsace, Edelzwicker, is a blend of many varieties. Its slightly spicy nose, lush fruit and bright acidity pairs very well with the Brown Butter Sauce and intense pumpkin flavor.

Brown Butter Sauce

⅓ cup Carrot Stock
   (see page 227)
1 pound butter, cubed
⅓ cup Brown Butter
   (see page 226)
Salt and pepper

Garnish

⅓ cup pumpkin seeds
⅓ cup butternut squash,
   small dice
2 tablespoons butter
Salt and pepper
1 tablespoon sage, chiffonade
1 cup truffled cheese, such as
   Perla Grigia al Tartufo, grated
   (optional)

When you cook the ravioli, make sure the water is at a
low simmer. If the water is boiling too rapidly, you risk
breaking the ravioli.

Hen Egg Truffle Ravioli Serves Six

For our honeymoon, Melissa and I toured the Northern Italian region of Barolo. One day, we spent all morning visiting the local vineyards and didn't finish until nearly 2 pm. For us that was lunchtime. The locals, however, had a different idea.

Most small village restaurants shut their doors around 1:30 pm and reopen later in the evening. We tried a few places, all of which turned us down. Desperate and hungry, we eventually ended up in a small restaurant on the edge of town. In my best broken Italian, I explained to the owner that we were touring the vineyards and lost track of time. The gentleman must have felt our despair because he let us in.

The restaurant was typical of what you would expect in a small Italian village: small, charming and family owned. We were escorted through the kitchen to a small alcove away from the main dining room. It was, I assumed, the area where the family ate. The space was small with only three tables, one of which was occupied by another couple, whom we discovered later to be the Italian ambassador of Spain. Needless to say, we were a little uncomfortable.

When the owner came to take our order, I said that we'd be thankful for whatever he gave us. We sat there for two hours and had six courses paired with the local wine. The most memorable dish was an egg ravioli with black truffles and ricotta cheese. When you cut into the center of the ravioli, the yolk luxuriously oozed out onto the plate. For the life of me, I couldn't figure out how this little restaurant fashioned such a lavish dish.

Years later, my chef de cuisine Dave Santos created a similar dish. When I first saw it, I couldn't believe my eyes. I was so excited that I grabbed Melissa, who was equally ecstatic. "We had this before! In Barolo, remember?" When Dave showed me how he made it, I was shocked at its simplicity.

Attempting this at home may take some practice. I suggest you have a few test runs before spending all that money on truffles. Once you master the technique, you'll be a superstar at your next dinner party. Notice the look on the faces of your guests as they cut into the pasta and break the yolk. Magnificent.

Fold the truffle oil into the ricotta and season the mix with salt and white pepper. Refrigerate until needed.

Flatten the pasta dough with the palm of your hand and run it through the pasta machine on its highest setting. Continue passing the pasta, lowering the dial after each pass. The sheet of pasta should be thin but not translucent.

Place the pasta dough across a lightly floured work surface. Trim the uneven ends off the pasta sheet. Cut the sheet widthwise into 2 pieces. One should be 4 to 5 inches longer than the other.

Place the ring mold in one corner of the shorter sheet but do not cut through the pasta. Spoon 2 tablespoons of the ricotta filling in the center of the ring mold. Continue with the remaining raviolis, leaving about an inch between each one. With a spoon, create a well in the ricotta and gently place a yolk inside each one.

Carefully lay the larger sheet of pasta over the smaller sheet. Be very careful not to break the yolks. With your fingers, press the top layer of dough into the bottom layer to create a seal around each ravioli. Place the dull end of the ring mold directly over each ravioli and press down to reinforce the seal. When the 2 layers of dough are thoroughly joined together, cut out the raviolis with

the ring mold. Transfer them to a sheet tray dusted with cornmeal to prevent sticking. Refrigerate until ready to cook.

In a medium-sized saucepot, reduce the Mushroom Stock by a quarter. Lower the heat and whisk in the cubes of butter, one at a time. Adjust the seasoning with salt and pepper. Keep warm until ready to use.

Note: This sauce is very fragile. If it sits too long, gets too hot, gets too cold, or if the butter isn't properly emulsified, it will break. It should be made right before serving.

Bring a large pot of salted water to a slow simmer. Drop the ravioli in the water and cook for 3 minutes. Divide the ravioli among 6 serving bowls and drizzle each portion with the Mushroom-Butter Sauce. Garnish the pasta with shaved black truffle and chives.

NOTES
SPECIAL EQUIPMENT: Pasta machine, 3-inch ring mold, truffle shaver.

 WINE PAIRING: Personal nostalgia aside, the Nebbiolo grape in Barolo has an earthiness that plays well with the flavors of black truffles.

INGREDIENTS

1⅓ cup ricotta cheese
½ teaspoon truffle oil
Pasta dough (see page 230)
All-purpose flour,
  as needed for dusting
6 hen egg yolks
1 cup cornmeal
8 ounces butter, cubed
½ cup Mushroom Stock
  (see page 229)
Salt and white pepper
1 black truffle, shaved
2 tablespoons chives,
  finely chopped

Barramundi with Pomegranate Reduction and Arugula Salad Serves Eight

People often ask me why we don't do lunch. The truth is we did in December 2006. When a new cook starts, we jokingly tell them that we stopped serving lunch after the last cook died. Well, not really, but it's not far from the truth.

Lunch was very successful. We were booked nearly every day. The problem was that my already overworked staff hated it. A large part of the success of the restaurant is due to my employees. I could see in their faces that the addition of lunch on top of dinner service was just too much. It was a big hand that I had to fold, but it was the right decision.

One positive that carried over from the short-lived lunch service was this barramundi dish. It always amazed me how many people loved this relatively simple dish. When the dust settled, we moved it over to the dinner menu.

This particular dish translates well for the home cook. When working with pomegranates, I would advise that you do not wear your Sunday best—it can be a messy process. When my cooks work with a large amount, they wear trash bags over their chef whites. The reduction can be omitted if you do not want to go through all the trouble, however the seeds are essential. They give the salad its crunch and a wonderful earthiness.

INGREDIENTS

Grapeseed oil
8 skin-on barramundi fillets, ap-
    proximately 6 ounces each
Salt

Pomegranate Reduction
5 pomegranates
    (for the reduction)
2 pomegranates (for the salad)
1 tablespoon sugar

Pickled Grapefruit
2 large ruby red grapefruits
1 cup Simple Syrup
    (see page 230)
½ cup Banyuls vinegar

Arugula Salad
1 pound arugula
2 Belgian endives, halved length-
    wise and sliced into
    1-inch pieces
1½ cups pomegranate seeds
Pickled Grapefruit supremes
    (from above)
Pomegranate Reduction
    (from above)
1 tablespoon extra-virgin olive oil
1 tablespoon grapefruit pickling
    liquid

POMEGRANATE REDUCTION

Slice 5 pomegranates in half widthwise. With the cut-side down, hold the fruit over a large bowl and lightly tap the back of it with a large spoon. The pomegranate seeds will release themselves from the shell. Discard any white pith that may have adhered to the seeds. Run the seeds through the food mill to extract the juice. The amount of juice may vary. In the end, there should be approximately 2–2½ cups of juice.

The remaining 2 pomegranates will be for the salad. Remove the seeds using the same procedure and reserve.

In a heavy-bottomed pot, bring the juice and sugar to a boil. Lower the heat to a simmer and reduce for approximately 1 hour until the mixture is slightly syrupy but not too thick. Strain and refrigerate the reduction until needed.

PICKLED GRAPEFRUIT

Using a sharp knife, peel the grapefruits leaving no pith on the outside of the fruit. Then remove each segment from the inner membrane. There should be no pith or membranes on the grapefruit "supremes." Halve each supreme widthwise and place in a bowl.

In a heavy-bottomed saucepot, bring the Simple Syrup and Banyuls vinegar to a boil. Pour the hot liquid over the grapefruit and let it steep at room temperature for 20 minutes. Cover and refrigerate.

ASSEMBLY

Heat a sauté pan over medium-high heat. When the pan is hot, coat the bottom with grapeseed oil. Season the flesh side of the fish fillets with salt. Carefully place the barramundi in the pan, skin-side down. You may need to do this in a few pans or in batches to prevent overcrowding the pan. The skin will immediately begin to curl up. Lightly press the flesh down with a fish spatula until the fillet begins to relax. Lower the heat to medium. Cook for approximately 3 minutes, turn the fillets over, and cook for an additional 2 minutes. Allow the fillets to rest on a layer of paper towels to remove any excess oil.

Place the arugula, endive, pomegranate seeds and pickled grapefruit in a large bowl. Toss with the olive oil and grapefruit pickling liquid. Adjust the seasoning with salt. It is important to assemble this right before serving or the salad may wilt.

To serve, pile 2 cups of the salad in the center of a large plate. Position the barramundi fillet, skin-side up, directly atop the salad. Drizzle the Pomegranate Reduction around the salad.

NOTES
SPECIAL EQUIPMENT: Food mill.

 WINE PAIRING: Chenin Blanc is a terrific complement to the grapefruit and pomegranate components of this dish. I particularly like the wines from Vouvray, located in the central part of the Loire Valley.

If barramundi is not available, any light fish can be substituted.

If searing the fish, note that the recipe calls for the fish to be cooked "skin-side" down. This refers to where the skin used to be on the fillet. This is done because the flesh is tighter on the skin side making it easier to cook.

Braised Atlantic Halibut with White Bean Broth and Fettuccini Serves Eight

When we originally created this dish, the halibut was poached in the broth. It makes for an easier preparation because it only requires one pot. This is one of those instances where, as a chef, I over thought the preparation trying to get the perfect flavors. We modified the recipe to seared halibut because people enjoy and identify with a crust on their fish. Try it both ways. You will see that poaching allows the true flavor of the halibut to come out. Follow the recipe procedure the same way. Poach the halibut in the broth at 140 degrees for about 6–8 minutes. Sprinkle the rosemary and orange zest on top of the cooked fish.

WHITE BEAN BROTH
Combine all ingredients in a large pot and simmer for 45 minutes. Strain the liquid through a chinois and discard the solids. Adjust the seasoning with salt and reserve.

GARNISH
In a large pot, sweat the bacon on low heat until most of the fat has rendered, about 10 minutes. Remove the bacon from the pot, leaving the rendered fat. Add the carrots and sweat for 5 minutes. Next add the celery and cook for 3 minutes. Then add the red onion, celery root and rosemary, and cook an additional 5 minutes or until tender, stirring often. Transfer the bacon back to the pot and deglaze with the orange juice. Cook until the most of the orange juice has evaporated, about 5 minutes. Remove vegetables and bacon from the pan and reserve.

FETTUCCINI
Flatten half of the pasta with the heel of your hand. Pass it through the pasta machine on its highest setting. Continue passing the pasta through, lowering the dial after each pass. If the sheet gets too long to handle comfortably, it can be cut in half. Each pasta sheet should be thin but not translucent.

Some pasta machines have a fettuccini attachment. If yours does not, the pasta can be cut by hand. Trim the uneven ends off the sheet and cut it into 10- to 12-inch lengths. With a sharp knife and a ruler, cut ¼-inch strips from each sheet. Place the pasta on a sheet tray dusted with flour. The fettuccini can be frozen until needed. Continue with the remaining pasta.

ASSEMBLY
Warm the garnish in 1 quart of the White Bean Broth. Stir in the orange juice.

Heat a sauté pan on medium heat and add the grapeseed oil. Meanwhile, bring a large pot of salted water to a boil for the pasta. Season the fillets on both sides with salt and pepper. Sear the fillets for 4 minutes on the skin side, flip and cook for an additional 4 minutes. Sprinkle the rosemary and orange zest on the presentation side of each fillet.

While the fish is cooking, add the pasta to the water and cook for 3 minutes. Strain, transfer to a bowl and toss with the butter to prevent it from sticking together.

Mound ½ cup of pasta in the center of a shallow bowl. Spoon ½ cup of the vegetables and broth over the pasta and top with the halibut.

NOTES
SPECIAL EQUIPMENT: Chinois or fine-mesh strainer, pasta machine.

 WINE PAIRING: For a rich sauce such as the bacon-bean broth, I like to pair wine that has rich fruit yet high acidity. Pinot Noir from Nuits St. George is an excellent choice.

INGREDIENTS

White Bean Broth
1 quart white cannelloni beans
3 quarts Chicken Stock
  (see page 227)
½ teaspoon fennel seeds
½ teaspoon coriander seeds
¼ teaspoon black peppercorns
2 cloves garlic, halved
½ ounce slab bacon
¼ white onion, chopped
½ celery rib, chopped
¼ cup leeks (white and pale
  green parts only), chopped
¼ cup carrot, chopped
1 sprig thyme
1 sprig rosemary
Salt

Garnish
½ cup slab bacon, medium dice
1 cup carrot, medium dice
1 cup celery, medium dice
1 cup celery root, medium dice
1½ cups red onion, medium dice
1 teaspoon rosemary, chopped
½ cup freshly squeezed orange
  juice

Fettuccini
Pasta dough (see page 230)
All-purpose flour

Halibut
8 halibut fillets (approximately 6
  ounces each)
Juice of 2 oranges
Zest of 2 oranges
1 tablespoon rosemary, chopped
Grapeseed oil
2 tablespoons butter
Salt and pepper

Smoked potatoes are a little more work than regular whipped potatoes, but the effort is worth it, especially when you taste them paired with this cod.

Cod with Smoked Potatoes and Pickled Honshimeji Mushrooms Serves Eight

While testing this recipe, we came to the realization that someone may burn their house to the ground attempting to rig up a stovetop smoker. Please don't be that person.

If you don't own a home smoker, I suggest you do this outdoors on a grill. If you choose to use a home smoker or rig one up on the stovetop, be careful. Be sure the oven fan works well and blows the exhaust outside or you may attract the fire department. It might also be a good idea to have a fire extinguisher nearby… just in case.

SMOKED POTATO PUREE

Place the potatoes in a large pot of cold, salted water. Bring the water up to a boil then lower the heat and simmer for 45 minutes to 1 hour, or until the potatoes are tender. A paring knife should be able to slide through to the center of a potato with little or no resistance.

Drain the potatoes and smoke for 10 minutes.

Note: If you do not own a home smoker, reference the Smoked Tomato Vinaigrette recipe on page 126 to construct one yourself.

Place the tamis over a large bowl and force the potatoes through using a plastic bowl scraper or rubber spatula. The skins will not pass through the mesh. Discard them after the potatoes have been passed. Stir the butter and milk into the potatoes until they are fully incorporated. The consistency should be quite loose. Add more warm milk, if needed. Season with salt.

Smoked Potato Puree can be made up to 2 days ahead and kept refrigerated. Reheat the potatoes on the stovetop. Stir in a little more milk to get the right consistency.

PICKLED HONSHIMEJI MUSHROOMS

Remove the mushroom caps with a pair of kitchen shears and place them in a metal bowl. Discard the stems.

Combine the water, vinegar and sugar in a medium-sized pot and bring to a boil. When the sugar has dissolved, pour the liquid over the mushrooms and let them steep in the pickling liquid at least 30 minutes. Refrigerate until needed.

RED PEPPER OIL

Place the red pepper juice in a saucepot and gently simmer for 1 hour. Strain the liquid and transfer to a clean pot. Continue to simmer the juice for another hour until it has reduced to syrup. This must be done slowly so the pepper juice doesn't burn. The entire process can take up to 3½ hours. Strain the syrup and whisk in the lemon oil and lemon juice. Transfer to a squeeze bottle and store in the refrigerator. Bring to room temperature before serving.

ASSEMBLY

Heat a large sauté pan over medium-high heat. Coat the bottom with grapeseed oil. Season each cod fillet with salt and pepper. Sear, skin-side up, for 1 minute. Lower the flame to medium. Add butter to the pan and baste the fillet with the hot butter. Cook for 3–4 minutes then turn the fillet over for an additional 1–2 minutes, continuously basting the fish. Remove the fillet from the pan and let it rest on a layer of paper towels.

Heat up the potatoes and the mushrooms on the stovetop. Spoon approximately ½ cup of the potatoes on the bottom of a shallow bowl. Spoon a thin ring of red pepper oil around the perimeter of the potatoes (you can also use a squeeze bottle) and scatter a few mushrooms around the oil. Sit the cod fillet in the center of the potatoes. Place a lemon supreme and a sprig of fried parsley on top of the fish.

NOTES

SPECIAL EQUIPMENT: Home smoker, fine-mesh tamis, electric fruit/vegetable juicer.

 WINE PAIRING: Chablis is the perfect match for the richness of the potatoes. Chablis has a perception problem in America because so many American producers of jug wine call their product "Chablis," though it has little resemblance to this fine French white.

INGREDIENTS

Smoked Potato Puree

6 Yukon Gold potatoes
8 ounces butter (2 sticks), room temperature
2 cups milk, warm

Pickled Honshimeji Mushrooms

2 bunches honshimeji (beech) mushrooms or any small mild mushroom
2 cups water
1 cup rice wine vinegar
½ cup sugar

Red Pepper Oil

8 red bell peppers, seeded and juiced
1 tablespoon lemon oil
1 teaspoon lemon juice

Cod

8 cod fillets (approximately 6 ounces each)
2 tablespoons grapeseed oil
2 tablespoons butter
Salt and pepper
Supremes from 1 lemon
Fried parsley for garnish

Butter Poached Lobster, Black-Truffle Mascarpone Agnolotti, Melted Leeks and Brown Butter Sauce Serves Eight

While most of the Restaurant Nicholas menu changes seasonally, lobster is a mainstay. The procedure for cooking the lobster is always the same, only the accompaniments vary with the availability of the freshest ingredients. This particular preparation was originally created for a winter truffle menu.

INGREDIENTS

Melted Leeks
4 medium leeks, white and pale
   green part only
½ cup butter
½ cup water
½ teaspoon salt
White pepper

Black-Truffle Mascarpone Filling
2 cups mascarpone
1 tablespoon truffle oil
1 teaspoon chopped black truffle
Salt and black pepper

Agnolotti
Pasta dough (see page 230)
All-purpose flour

Lobsters
6 lobsters, approximately 1½
   pounds each
4 cups Beurre Monté
   (see page 226)
½ cup kosher salt
¼ cup red wine vinegar
1 gallon water

MELTED LEEKS
Cut each leek in half lengthwise and remove the center layer from each half. Portion each half into approximately 4-inch pieces and slice lengthwise into a large julienne. After all the leeks are cut, wash thoroughly in cold water and dry.

Combine the water and butter in a large pot and heat on medium-low until the butter has melted. Add the leeks and cook for approximately 10 minutes, stirring frequently to avoid browning. Season with salt and pepper, and reserve.

BLACK-TRUFFLE MASCARPONE FILLING
In a medium-size bowl, whisk all the ingredients together until soft. Transfer the mixture into the piping bag.

AGNOLOTTI
Divide the pasta dough into three separate pieces and cover each with plastic wrap. With the heel of your hand, flatten one of the portions to a size that will fit into your pasta machine. On the highest setting, pass the pasta through twice. Lower the setting one notch and pass the dough through 2 more times. Then fold the long ends into the center and press down with the heel of your hand to make the dough into a rectangle. Pass the dough through the machine with the folded crease vertical. Continue passing the dough through, lowering the dial until the pasta is a thin sheet but not translucent. Position the sheet in front of you horizontally. Be sure your work surface is lightly floured or the dough may stick. If the dough feels too sticky, dust it with flour before passing it through the pasta machine.

Cut the sheet of dough in half lengthwise so there are 2 long sheets of dough, each piece about 3 inches wide. Trim the ends of each piece to make them relatively equal in size. Pipe a long strip of filling directly across the middle of each sheet. Take the bottom edge of each sheet and fold it over the filling to meet up with the top edge. Working from one end, gently press the top of the filling to push out any air bubbles and create a seal.

Start at one end of the sheet. Using your thumb and forefingers, pinch a pillow about 1 inch wide out of the filling by squeezing your fingers together and gently pushing inward.

Continue until both sheets have small pillows, each ¾ inch apart. With a crimped pastry wheel, trim off the remaining dough about ½ inch from the top of the pillow. Carefully slide a small offset spatula underneath the dough to release it from the work surface. Cut out the individual agnolotti by running the pastry wheel vertically between the pieces.

Place the finished product on a floured sheet pan. If using immediately, refrigerate until ready to cook. The pasta can also be frozen. If you choose to freeze the agnolotti, first freeze them laying flat on a tray. When they are completely frozen, they can be stored in freezer bags. If the pasta is placed into the freezer bags before it is completely frozen, the pieces will stick together as they freeze.

LOBSTERS
In a large stockpot, bring water, salt and vinegar to a rolling boil. Meanwhile, carefully remove the tail and claws from each lobster. You might want to wear rubber gloves to protect your hands from the lobsters' sharp spines. The bodies can be frozen and used for other applications, such as lobster stock.

Separate the tails, pincher claws and crusher claws (larger of the 2 claws). Cook the tails in boiling water for 1½ minutes and immediately transfer them to a large ice bath. Repeat the process with the pincher claws (4½ minutes) and crushers (5½ minutes). The lobster should stay in the ice bath until cooled completely, up to 10 minutes. The claws and tails will not be fully cooked.

With a sharp, heavy chef's knife, split the tails lengthwise and remove each piece of meat from the shell. Rinse under cold water to remove the vein and any roe. For the claws, remove the lobster "knuckle," or arm, from each claw. To remove the meat from the knuckle, simply cut through the

continues »

When you bite into the agnolotti, an intense truffle flavor explodes in your mouth. However, if you don't have the time to make the agnolotti, the filling can be spooned in the center of the plate to melt with the leeks.

shell with a pair of kitchen shears. Remove the meat and rinse it under cold water. You can add the knuckle meat to this dish or reserve it for another application.

Next detach the small, moveable part of the claw, being careful to also remove the thin piece of cartilage. If the cartilage breaks off inside the claw, it can be removed after the meat is out of the shell. Hold the claw flat on a cutting board and gently tap it with the back of the knife until it cracks. Remove the meat in one piece and rinse off any of the white substance that may remain.

BROWN BUTTER SAUCE

Melt the Carrot Stock over medium heat. When it just begins to boil, lower the flame and whisk in the cubes of butter, one at a time. Be careful. If the flame is too high or too low, the butter will not emulsify properly with the Carrot Stock and the sauce will break. Add the Brown Butter and continue whisking until incorporated completely. The sauce should be light, homogenous and creamy. Season with salt and pepper. This sauce is very fragile. It needs to be kept warm— but not hot—until ready to use. To be safe, make it just before serving.

ASSEMBLY

To completely cook the lobster, heat the Beurre Monté until barely simmering, then reduce the flame to its lowest setting. If the Beurre Monté boils or gets too hot, it may break. Add the lobster claws and tails and gently poach them for 7 minutes. Meanwhile, submerge the agnolotti in boiling salted water until the pieces float, about 2–3 minutes. For frozen pasta, cook a minute longer. Drain the pasta and toss it with a small amount of Brown Butter Sauce to prevent it from sticking together.

Spoon ⅓ cup of warm Melted Leeks in the center of a shallow bowl. Interlock the lobster portions (1 of each claw and the 2 tail halves) and place them on the leeks. Arrange about 5 agnolotti around the lobster and spoon 2–3 tablespoons of Brown Butter Sauce over the top.

NOTES

SPECIAL EQUIPMENT: Pasta machine, crimped pastry wheel, small offset spatula, pastry piping bag with ½-inch plain tip.

 WINE PAIRING: This dish was made to go with a full, buttery California Chardonnay. Warmer climates, like the Napa Valley, best produce this type of wine.

Brown Butter Sauce
⅓ cup Carrot Stock
  (see page 227)
1 pound butter, cubed
⅓ cup Brown Butter
  (see page 226)
Salt and black pepper

Butter Poached Lobster
with Pickled Ramps and Lemon Pappardelle

Cleaning two bunches of ramps, as are called for in this recipe, can be a messy, dirty, slimy process—there's no easy way around it. And even when you've finished cleaning them, their pungent odor can remain on your hands for up to a day. (Try washing with lemon juice.)

It's all worthwhile, however, when you taste how delicious freshly pickled ramps can be. At the restaurant, we pickle nearly 70 pounds at a time. After the third or fourth night of staying late to clean and pickle the delicate little plants, my weary kitchen crew ponders the existence of God. And you're worried about two bunches...

If two bunches seem like child's play, however, you can pickle a larger batch—maybe not 70 pounds—and use them for salads and vegetable dishes throughout the year.

INGREDIENTS

Pappardelle

6 egg yolks

1 whole egg

Zest of 2 lemons

2 cups all-purpose flour

1 teaspoon extra-virgin olive oil

1 teaspoon milk

1 tablespoon lemon oil

Pickled Ramps

2 bunches ramps

2 cups water

1 cup red wine vinegar

1 cup sugar

1 sprig thyme

1 clove garlic

5 black peppercorns

1 bay leaf

Lobsters

6 lobsters, approximately 1½
   pounds each

4 cups Beurre Monté
   (see page 226)

½ cup kosher salt

¼ cup red wine vinegar

1 gallon water

PAPPARDELLE

In a large bowl or directly on a clean work surface, mound the flour and create a small well in the center with your fingers. Add the yolks and whole egg, zest, milk and oil into the well and slowly stir to incorporate the flour. Knead the dough until smooth, about 10 minutes. Divide the dough into thirds and let it rest in freezer bags or plastic wrap for 30 minutes.

Working in batches, flatten the dough with the palm of your hand and run each piece through the pasta machine on its widest setting. After each pass, lower the setting until the pasta is very thin but not translucent. The sheets can be cut in half for easier handling.

Place a sheet of pasta in front of you horizontally. Trim the uneven ends with a sharp knife. With a crimped pastry wheel, cut 1-inch vertical pieces from the sheet. Lay the pieces on a sheet tray lined with parchment paper and dusted with flour. It is important that the pieces don't touch each other. Freeze the pasta until ready to use.

PICKLED RAMPS

Remove the top green portion and trim the root off the bulb end of each ramp. Use a towel to remove the top layer of skin—it should rub right off. Rinse the ramps under cold water to remove any dirt.

Make a bouquet garni by placing the thyme, garlic, peppercorns and bay leaf in a piece of cheesecloth. Gather the edges of the cheesecloth together and tie the satchel up with butcher's twine.

Combine the water, vinegar, sugar and bouquet garni in a large pot and bring it to a boil. Add the ramps and remove the pot from the heat. Let the ramps steep in the pickling liquid until they are cool enough to go into the refrigerator. When completely cool, cut into 1-inch pieces.

LOBSTERS

In a large stockpot, bring water, salt and vinegar to a rolling boil. Meanwhile, carefully remove the tail and claws from each lobster. You might want to wear rubber gloves to protect your hands from the lobsters' sharp spines.

continues »

Ramps are wild onions available in
the early spring.

Separate the tails, pincher claws and crusher claws (larger of the 2 claws). The bodies can be frozen and used for other applications, such as lobster stock. Cook the tails in boiling water for 1½ minutes, then immediately transfer them to a large ice bath. Repeat the process with the pincher claws (4½ minutes) and crushers (5½ minutes). The lobster should stay in the ice bath until completely cooled, up to 10 minutes. The claws and tails will not be fully cooked.

With a sharp, heavy chef's knife, split the tails lengthwise and remove each piece of meat from the shell. Rinse the meat under cold water to remove the vein and any roe. For the claws, remove the lobster "knuckle," or arm, from each claw and reserve them for another use.

Detach the small, moveable part of the claw, being careful to also remove the thin piece of cartilage. If the cartilage breaks off inside the claw, it can be removed after the meat is out of the shell. Hold the claw flat on a cutting board and gently tap it with the back of the knife until it cracks. Remove the meat in one piece and rinse off any of the white substance that may remain.

SHERRY BUTTER SAUCE
Melt the Carrot Stock over medium heat. When it just begins to boil, lower the flame and whisk in the cubes of butter, one at a time. Be careful. If the flame is too high or too low, the butter will not emulsify properly with the Carrot Stock and the sauce will break. Add the sherry and continue whisking until incorporated completely. The sauce should be light, homogenous and creamy. Season with salt and pepper. This sauce is very fragile. It needs to be kept warm—but not hot—until ready to use. To be safe, make it just before serving.

SNAP PEAS
Bring a large pot of salted water to a boil. Add the snap peas and cook for 25 seconds. Remove the peas from the water and shock them in an ice bath. Remove the tough fiber that runs down the seam of each pea pod and pull the pod in half.

ASSEMBLY
Bring a large pot of salted water to a boil. To finish cooking the lobsters, heat the Beurre Monté until barely simmering, then reduce the flame to its lowest setting. Add the lobster meat and gently poach for 7 minutes. Meanwhile, submerge the pappardelle in the boiling water for 3 minutes. Drain and toss it with lemon oil to prevent it from sticking together.

In a medium saucepot, warm the snap peas and ramps in 1 tablespoon of the Sherry Butter Sauce. Twirl the pappardelle on a meat fork and place the bundle in the center of a plate. Interlock a portion of lobster (1 of each claw and 2 tail halves) and sit it on the pasta. Spoon the vegetables around the plate. Ladle the sauce over the lobster.

NOTES
SPECIAL EQUIPMENT: Pasta machine, crimped pastry wheel, cheesecloth, butcher's twine.

 WINE PAIRING: Typically Chardonnay from Chablis, in northern Burgundy, is aged mostly in stainless steel or neutral oak. This makes for a crisp, racy wine, which will match nicely with the spring flavors of this dish.

Sherry Butter Sauce
1 pound butter, cubed
½ cup Carrot Stock
  (see page 227)
2 tablespoons good quality
  cream sherry
Salt and black pepper

Snap Peas
2 cups snap peas

Any light fish can be substituted for the sea bass, with or without the skin.

Crusted Black Sea Bass with Banyuls Broth _Serves Eight_

This is my all-time favorite fish dish. It is fairly easy to prepare and packed with flavor. Banyuls vinegar can be found at most high-end food stores. The bass is cooked with the skin on, which will take some technique and finesse.

BANYULS BROTH

In a saucepot, sauté the mushrooms in butter over medium-high heat. The mushrooms are done when most of the moisture cooks out and they reach a golden brown color.

Add the rest of the ingredients to the mushrooms and season with salt and pepper. Simmer for 45 minutes. Strain through a chinois and discard the mushrooms. Adjust the seasoning with salt, if needed, and reserve.

SPICE MIX

Grind all ingredients separately in the coffee/spice grinder. Mix together.

ASSEMBLY

Season the flesh side of each fillet with salt and pepper. With a pastry brush, baste the flesh side with heavy cream, then dip it into the spice mixture. It is important not to get any of the spice mixture on the skin side. Sprinkle flour on the skin side and shake off any excess.

Heat a sauté pan on medium-high heat and add the grapeseed oil. When the oil is hot, place the fillets in the pan, skin-side down. Do not overcrowd the pan. If necessary, use 2 pans or cook in batches. The fillets will start to curl. With a spatula, gently press the fish down into the pan until the fillets eventually relax. Cook the fillets until the skin is crispy and golden brown. Turn them over and cook on low heat for an additional 2 minutes.

While the fillets are cooking, bring the Banyuls Broth up to a boil, turn off the heat and whisk in the Brown Butter. When the butter is melted, stir in the herbs.

Serve each fillet with $1/2$ cup of the finished broth. In the restaurant, this dish is accompanied by cherry tomatoes, salsify and haricot verts.

NOTES

SPECIAL EQUIPMENT: Electric coffee/spice grinder, chinois or fine-mesh strainer.

 WINE PAIRING: In this instance, I prefer a red wine to a white one due to the intensity of the broth. Try a fruity California Pinot Noir.

INGREDIENTS

Banyuls Broth

$2\frac{1}{2}$ pounds white button mushrooms, washed and thinly sliced
¼ cup honey
¼ cup light soy sauce
¼ cup Banyuls vinegar
¼ cup lemon juice
1 quart water
3 tablespoons butter
Salt and pepper

Spice Mix

4 ounces almonds, toasted
4 ounces hazelnuts, toasted
4 ounces coriander seeds, toasted
4 ounces sesame seeds, toasted
1 ounce black peppercorns

Black Sea Bass

8 skin-on black sea bass fillets
   (approximately 6 ounces each)
½ cup heavy cream
½ cup Wondra flour
¼ cup Brown Butter
   (see page 226)
¼ cup oregano, chopped
¼ cup tarragon, chopped
1 tablespoon grapeseed oil
Salt and pepper

Halibut with Cauliflower Puree and Morels Serves Eight

INGREDIENTS

8 ounces morel mushrooms (or
    your favorite mushrooms)
1 large cauliflower
4 ounces butter
1 pound fresh fava beans in pods
Salt

Lemon-Caper Sauce
¼ cup capers, rough chopped
3 lemons, supremed and rough
    chopped
¼ cup Carrot Stock
    (see page 227)
1 teaspoon parsley, chopped
8 ounces cold butter (2 sticks),
    cubed
3 tablespoons Brown Butter
    (see page 226)

Halibut
8 halibut fillets (approximately 6
    ounces each)
1 cup panko breadcrumbs, finely
    ground in food processor
1 cup heavy cream
Salt and black pepper
Grapeseed oil

To clean the morels, remove and discard the bottom stem from each mushroom. Submerge the caps in cold water and gently agitate. Lift the mushrooms out and discard the water. Repeat this process 3 or 4 times until the mushrooms are completely cleaned. Place the mushrooms on a sheet pan lined with a rack to dry.

Meanwhile, bring a large pot of salted water to a boil. Cut the head of cauliflower down the center and remove and discard the stem. Slice the cauliflower into small pieces and blanch for 4 minutes. Drain. Transfer the florets to a blender. Add the butter and puree for 2 minutes or until it is completely smooth. Work in batches if necessary. Season with salt. Keep warm and reserve.

Bring a large pot of water to a boil. Separate the fava beans from the pods. Blanch the beans for 15 seconds then immediately shock them in an ice bath. Remove the beans from the ice bath and slip off the outer layer of skin from each bean. Discard the skins and reserve the beans.

When the morels are dry, cut them into ½-inch pieces. This may mean halved or quartered since the morels are larger toward the end of their growing season.

LEMON-CAPER SAUCE
Melt the Carrot Stock in a saucepot over medium heat. Whisk in the cubes of butter, 1 or 2 at a time. When the butter has melted and is emulsified into the stock, whisk in the brown butter. Turn off the heat. Right before serving, stir in the parsley, capers and lemons. This sauce should be made as close to serving as possible.

ASSEMBLY
Preheat the oven to 400 degrees. Thoroughly dry each fillet with paper towels then season each side with salt. Brush a thin layer of heavy cream on the cleaner side (usually the skin side) of the fish, then dip it in the panko. Shake off any excess crumbs.

Heat a large sauté pan on medium heat. Coat the bottom with a thin layer of grapeseed oil. Place the fish in the pan, breaded side down, and cook for 1–2 minutes or until the breadcrumbs are slightly brown. Work in batches so you don't overcrowd the pan. Transfer the fish to a sheet pan, breaded side up, and place in the oven. Depending on the thickness of the fillet, the cooking time can take 2–5 minutes.

To check for doneness, pierce the thickest part of the fillet with a thin metal skewer or cake tester. Hold for 10 seconds, remove the skewer, and press it underneath your bottom lip. The skewer should be warm but not hot. Before serving, place the fish on a layer of paper towels to remove any excess oil.

Meanwhile, heat a sauté pan on medium heat and coat the bottom with grapeseed oil. When the oil is hot, add the morels and sauté for 2 minutes. Add the fava beans just to warm through. Season with salt and pepper.

Spoon approximately ⅓ cup of the cauliflower puree in the center of a plate. Gingerly spread it out with the back of a spoon to form a circle. Place the fish atop the puree, breaded side up. Spoon the morels and fava beans around the fish. Drizzle the desired amount of Lemon-Caper Sauce on and around the halibut.

NOTES
 WINE PAIRING: Russian River Chardonnay is rich yet vibrant. It is the perfect pairing with the Lemon-Caper Sauce.

If fava beans or morels are out of season, substitute peas and whatever variety of mushroom is available. Any mild white fish, such as bass or cod, can be used in the place of the halibut.

Used widely in Japanese cuisine, kombu can be found at most Asian markets. We use madai fillets for this dish to keep with the Japanese theme. Bass or red snapper will yield similar results.

Madai with Miso Broth Serves Eight

MISO BROTH
Bring the water and kombu up to a simmer. Remove from heat and steep for 1 hour. Return broth to the stovetop and add the ginger and lemongrass. Gently simmer for 45 minutes. Strain the broth and discard the solids. Whisk in the remaining ingredients. The broth may need more miso or vinegar. Taste and adjust seasoning.

ORANGE-SOY MARINADE
Whisk all ingredients together. Reserve.

SUSHI RICE
Place the sushi rice in a large bowl and soak under slowly running cold water for 30 minutes. Drain. Cook in the rice cooker using the manufacturer's instructions.

When the rice is finished, allow it to rest for 10 minutes. Fold in the rice wine vinegar and mirin. Adjust the seasoning with salt and sugar. Keep warm until ready to use.

ASSEMBLY
Heat a pot large enough to hold the rice on medium heat. Coat the bottom with grapeseed oil. Sauté the bok choy and soy beans for 30 seconds. Gently stir in the rice and coat with approximately ⅓ cup of the orange marinade. Cook for 1 minute and set aside.

Heat a heavy-bottomed sauté pan on medium-high heat. Coat the bottom with grapeseed oil. Dry each piece of fish with paper towels. Season the flesh with salt and pepper.

Carefully place the fillets into the hot oil, skin-side down. Do not overcrowd the pan. Cook in batches, if necessary. The fish will immediately curl up so gently press the fillets down with a spatula. When they eventually relax, lower the heat to medium and cook until the skin becomes golden brown and crispy. Turn the fish over and cook for an additional 2 minutes.

Serve the fillets over a bed of sushi rice. Pour the miso broth around the rice.

NOTES
SPECIAL EQUIPMENT: Rice cooker.

 WINE PAIRING: Alsatian Riesling tends to be bone dry and full bodied. The powerful fruit will stand up to the ginger and soy. Be sure your selection is dry; a sweeter wine will bring out the fishiness in the broth.

INGREDIENTS

Miso Broth
½ ounce kombu
1 quart water
½ stalk lemongrass, chopped
1 tablespoon ginger
1 tablespoon miso paste
1 teaspoon mirin
2 teaspoons rice wine vinegar

Orange-Soy Marinade
1 cup fresh orange juice
3 tablespoons mirin
2 tablespoons honey
¼ cup soy sauce
2 tablespoons sesame oil

Sushi Rice
2 cups sushi rice
2 cups water
½ cup mirin
½ cup rice wine vinegar
Sugar and salt

Madai
8 madai fillets (approximately 6 ounces each)
Grapeseed oil
¼ cup bok choy stems, medium dice
¼ cup soy beans, medium dice
Salt and pepper

Pan Roasted Salmon with
Summer Bean Salad and Smoked Tomato Vinaigrette Serves Six

The Smoked Tomato Vinaigrette is the star of this dish. It makes the salmon taste as if it had been slightly smoked. This is not the easiest recipe to master—one way or another, you're going to have to set up some sort of smoker. I suggest you attempt this outdoors on the grill rather than in your home. It's much safer. If you do try this in your kitchen, please be careful. Be sure your kitchen fan works and try not to burn your house down.

INGREDIENTS

Smoked Tomato Vinaigrette
4–5 Roma tomatoes, halved lengthwise
¼ cup red wine vinegar
1½ cups extra-virgin olive oil
1 tablespoon salt
1 tablespoon plus 1 teaspoon sugar
3 cups cherry wood chips

Summer Bean Salad
8 ounces green Romano beans
8 ounces yellow Romano beans
8 ounces haricot verts
8 ounces yellow wax beans

Oven-dried Tomatoes
2 cups grape tomatoes
1 teaspoon powdered sugar

Salmon
6 salmon fillets (approximately 6 ounces each)
2 tablespoons grapeseed oil
Salt and white pepper
¼ cup extra-virgin olive oil

SMOKED TOMATO VINAIGRETTE (YIELDS 3 CUPS)

Pile the wood chips on one side of a roasting pan and ignite them with the blowtorch. Make sure your oven hood is on high, otherwise smoke damage may occur. Place the tomatoes, skin-side up, on a baking rack that fits directly into the roasting pan. Do not put the tomatoes directly over the open flame. The end opposite the wood chips may need to be propped up with something heat resistant, such as ovenproof ramekins.

Immediately cover the roasting pan with foil. Place the side of pan that contains the wood chips directly over a low flame. Smoke for 20–30 minutes or until the skins easily slide off the tomatoes. Remove the tomatoes and carefully extinguish the wood chips and discard them along with the tomato skins.

Note: This is how we do it at the restaurant, although it can easily be done outdoors on the grill. Heat one side of the grill on low while leaving the other side off. Place the wood chips in a disposable aluminum roasting pan, ignite them with the torch, and set the pan over the hot side of the grill. Lay the tomatoes, skin-side up, on a sheet pan set on the cool side of the grill. Close the lid and smoke the tomatoes until the skins slide off.

Place the smoked tomatoes and vinegar in a blender. Blend on high and slowly add the olive oil in a thin, steady stream. Season with salt and sugar and refrigerate. If the vinaigrette separates, a vigorous whisk will bring it back together. The vinaigrette will keep refrigerated for up to a week.

SUMMER BEAN SALAD

Remove both ends of each bean with a paring knife. In a large pot of boiling, salted water, blanch each bean variety separately until the desired doneness is achieved (about 2 minutes for al dente). Immediately shock in an ice bath. Each bean variety has a different cooking time, so check each batch for doneness and don't rely on time. Cook the yellow beans before the green ones so the water doesn't discolor. When all the beans have been blanched and shocked, cut each one in half on the bias. Reserve.

OVEN-DRIED TOMATOES

Toss tomatoes with sugar in a bowl and lay out on a sheet pan lined with parchment. Place the sheet pan in a 150-degree oven for 8 hours or until tomatoes are well shriveled but not completely dried out and hard. Tomatoes can be dried and then refrigerated for up to 5 days.

ASSEMBLY

Season both sides of each salmon fillet with salt and pepper. Heat the grapeseed oil in a sauté pan over medium heat. When oil is hot but not smoking, carefully lay fish, flesh-side down, in the pan and cook for 3–4 minutes or until a golden-brown crust forms and the fish releases itself from the pan. Flip the fillet and cook for an additional 2–3 minutes until desired doneness.

Toss the beans and dried tomatoes with olive oil. Season with salt and pepper.

Spoon or ladle a small amount of vinaigrette in the center of a plate to form a circle about 4 inches in diameter. Place ½ cup of bean salad in center of vinaigrette and sit salmon on top of the beans.

NOTES

SPECIAL EQUIPMENT: Propane blowtorch or a home smoker.

 WINE PAIRING: The gravelly soil of the Graves region of Bordeaux is home to some of the most unique Sauvignon-Blanc-based blends in the world. The smoky, flinty nature of these whites is a natural match for the smokiness of the tomato vinaigrette.

You can also omit the salmon and serve the beans and vinaigrette on their own as a light summer salad.

Skate with Brioche Crust and Tamarind-Curry Sauce Serves Six

TAMARIND-CURRY BROTH

In a dry sauté pan, lightly toast the curry on low heat for about 2 minutes. Remove from the pan and set aside. In a medium-sized saucepot, combine the coconut milk, chicken stock, chili, ginger, garlic and curry powder. Season with salt and simmer for 1 hour.

Remove broth from the heat and stir in tamarind paste until it completely dissolves. Strain the broth and discard the solids. The lime juice will be added right before serving.

JASMINE RICE

Thoroughly rinse the rice in a sieve or fine-mesh strainer by agitating the grains with your fingers until the water changes from milky to clear. Combine the rice and water in a saucepot and bring it to a boil. Lower the heat, cover, and simmer for 20 minutes. Remove the pot from the heat and let the rice rest covered for an additional 10 minutes. Fluff with a fork.

In a saucepot large enough to hold the rice, heat the grapeseed oil on medium heat. Sweat the red pepper for about 2 minutes. Season with salt. Add the haricot verts and stir just to warm them through. Mix in the rice. Adjust the seasoning with salt and pepper.

ASSEMBLY

Preheat the oven to 400 degrees. Season both sides of each skate fillet with salt and pepper. With the bloodline-side down, place a slice of brioche on each fillet.

Either cook the fish in batches or use multiple pans to prevent overcrowding. Heat 1 tablespoon of grapeseed oil in a sauté pan on medium-high heat. When the oil is hot, add 1 tablespoon of butter. Once the butter's frothing subsides, place the fish in the pan, brioche-side down, and transfer the pan to the oven for 3 minutes.

Return the pan to the stovetop and carefully turn the fish over. Cook over medium heat for an additional 2 minutes. Remove the fish from the pan and allow it to rest on a layer of paper towels.

Spoon ¾ cup of the rice in the center of each plate. Place the skate directly on top. Stir the lime juice into the broth and ladle about ¼ cup of it around the fish.

NOTES

WINE PAIRING: Pair this bold flavored skate dish with a Pinot Gris from Alsace. Choose one that has hints of fruit but is not overly sweet.

INGREDIENTS

Tamarind-Curry Broth
1 13½-ounce can coconut milk
1 cup Chicken Stock
   (see page 227)
½ Thai chili, split lengthwise
1 tablespoon ginger, peeled and
   rough chopped
1 clove garlic, rough chopped
½ tablespoon curry powder
1½ tablespoons tamarind paste
1 lime, juiced
Salt

Jasmine Rice
2 cups jasmine rice
2½ cups water
1 cup red bell pepper, small dice
1 cup haricot verts, blanched,
   shocked and small dice
1 tablespoon grapeseed oil
Salt and pepper

Skate
6 skate wing fillets (approximately
   6 ounces each)
6 slices brioche (¼ inch thick)
6 tablespoons grapeseed oil
6 tablespoons butter
Salt and pepper

Fennel Crusted Tuna with Tabouleh and Citrus Vinaigrette Serves Six

INGREDIENTS

Citrus Vinaigrette

6 oranges plus ½ orange, juiced
6 limes plus 3 limes, juiced
6 lemons plus 2 lemons, juiced
2 tablespoons fennel seed
2 whole star anise
2 tablespoons coriander seed
¼ teaspoon crushed red pepper
2 shallots, sliced
4 cloves garlic, sliced
1 tablespoon ginger, chopped
¼ cup rice wine vinegar
½ cup plus 2½ tablespoons sugar
2 egg yolks
Zest of 3 limes
1 cup grapeseed oil

Fennel-Pepper Crust

¼ cup fennel seed
¼ cup white peppercorns
½ teaspoon coriander seed
½ teaspoon cumin seed
2 bay leaves

Tabouleh Salad

2 cups quinoa
¼ cup red pepper, small dice
¼ cup cucumber, small dice
¼ cup fennel, small dice
¼ cup cucumber, small dice
2 whole Roma tomatoes
¼ cup zucchini, small dice
¼ cup celery, small dice
¼ cup mint, chiffonade
¼ cup parsley, chiffonade
1 lemon, juiced
4 tablespoons extra-virgin
   olive oil
Salt and pepper

Tuna

8 6-ounce blocks sushi-grade
   tuna, cleaned of bloodlines
   and sinew
Salt

CITRUS VINAIGRETTE

Combine the fennel seed, star anise, coriander seed, red pepper, shallots, garlic, ginger, vinegar, ½ cup of sugar, and juice of 6 oranges, 6 limes and 6 lemons in a saucepot. Simmer for 2 hours or until it is reduced by half. Strain the liquid and let cool in the refrigerator.

Transfer the cooled juice mixture to a blender. Add the egg yolks and 2½ tablespoons of sugar. With the blender on high, slowly drizzle in the grapeseed oil. After the oil is incorporated, add the remaining citrus juices. Pour the vinaigrette into a bowl and stir in the lime zest. Reserve.

FENNEL-PEPPER CRUST

Toast the spices in a dry saucepan over medium heat, tossing often, until the seeds are light brown and begin to pop. Grind into a powder.

TABOULEH SALAD

Combine the quinoa and 1 gallon of lightly salted water in a large pot and bring to a boil. Lower the heat and simmer for 30 minutes or until the kernels are tender. Strain and rinse under cold water. Reserve.

Bring a large pot of salted water to a boil. Slice the stem end off the tomatoes and score an "X" in the other end. Submerge them in the water for 15–30 seconds or until the skin begins to peel away from the "X." Immediately transfer to an ice bath. Allow the tomatoes to cool completely then remove the skins. Stand the tomatoes upright, cut into quarters, and fillet the seeds from each petal. Place the petals between 2 paper towels to remove excess moisture. Cut into a small dice and reserve.

In the same pot of water, add the zucchini and cook for 15 seconds. Drain and immediately transfer to an ice bath. Reserve.

Combine the diced vegetables and the quinoa in a large bowl. Drizzle with olive oil and lemon juice. Add the herbs and season with salt and pepper. Reserve.

Note: The Tabouleh Salad must be made the day it is to be served. After that, the herbs will look dull and the flavors go flat.

ASSEMBLY

Season the tuna with salt on all sides then roll it in the spice mixture. Heat a nonstick sauté pan on medium-high heat. Sear the tuna for 10 seconds on each side. Remove it from the pan and let it rest. This can be done in batches. Be sure to wipe out the pan after each batch.

Note: It is essential that the tuna is of superior quality. Bluefin tuna is ideal, although rare and very expensive. Yellowfin, which is less expensive and much more accessible, works just as well.

To finish, place approximately ¾ cup of tabouleh in the middle of a plate. With a sharp serrated knife, cut the tuna in ½-inch slices against the grain of the flesh. Shingle the slices on top of the salad and drizzle the vinaigrette on and around the fish. Garnish with a few strands of parsley and mint chiffonade.

NOTES

SPECIAL EQUIPMENT: Spice grinder.

 WINE PAIRING: This dish was made for summer. Sparkling Riesling from Germany, called Sekt, makes for a fun pairing. The bubbles really bring out the complexity of the spices.

The Tabouleh Salad will make a nice accompaniment for most fish. It can also be served on its own as a light, healthy lunch.

Juicing beets is a messy process. You should wear an apron and rubber gloves. When you are finished, your kitchen may look like a crime scene.

Salmon with Beet Jus and Horseradish Cream Serves Eight

Verjus, or verjuice, is an acidic juice made from unripe wine grapes. It's not the easiest find. Try Whole Foods or Dean & Deluca. If you cannot find verjus, a mixture of white grape juice and white wine vinegar can be substituted. The Beet Jus in this dish is very strong, so only a full-flavored fish like salmon can stand up to it.

BEET JUS

Combine all ingredients in a large, heavy-bottomed pot and bring to a boil. Reduce heat and simmer for 90 minutes. Be careful not to scorch the sides of the pot. Strain the liquid into a clean pot and discard the solids.

Continue reducing the liquid, straining every hour into a clean pot. This can take a few hours Keep in mind that the lower and slower the liquid reduces, the rounder and smoother the final product will be. When the liquid reaches a light syrup consistency, remove it from the heat. Strain it one final time and cool.

HORSERADISH CREAM

Combine the ingredients in a saucepot and bring to a boil. Reduce heat and simmer for 25 minutes. Season with salt and pepper. Strain sauce and reserve.

TOASTED CAULIFLOWER

Bring a large pot of salted water to a boil. Remove outer leaves from the cauliflower and submerge the head in the water. Cook until tender, about 5 minutes. Remove the cauliflower from the pot and shock it in ice water.

When the cauliflower has cooled, slice it into 1-inch pieces. For the slices closer to the center, remove the center stem.

Heat a sauté pan on medium heat and add the grapeseed oil. When the oil is hot, add the cauliflower slices. Let the cauliflower cook for 5 minutes on one side. When the seared side is golden brown, flip it over and add the butter, salt and pepper. Baste the brown side with the frothy butter. Continue cooking for an additional 3 minutes. Remove from pan and dry on paper towels.

ASSEMBLY

Season each salmon fillet with salt and pepper. Sprinkle thyme leaves on the cleaner side of each fillet. Heat a sauté pan on medium-high heat and add 1 tablespoon of grapeseed oil. When oil is hot, add the fillets, thyme-side down. To prevent overcrowding, do this in batches or multiple pans. Cook the fillets for 4 minutes or until the seared side is golden brown. Turn them over and cook for an additional 2 minutes. Remove from pan and rest on paper towels to remove excess oil.

Gently heat cream sauce until hot but not boiling. Add the crème fraîche and froth with an immersion blender.

Place a slice of the Toasted Cauliflower in the center of the plate. Drizzle the Beet Jus around the cauliflower, followed by a drizzle of lemon oil. Set the salmon directly on top of the cauliflower. Finish with the frothed Horseradish Cream and a few chive batons.

NOTES

SPECIAL EQUIPMENT: Immersion blender, electric fruit/vegetable juicer.

 WINE PAIRING: Salmon is one of those fish that pairs better with red wine than white. An American Pinot Noir has the right amount of fruit and acidity to stand up to the beets yet will not overpower the fish. Try something from Oregon's Willamette Valley.

INGREDIENTS

Beet Jus
15 red beets (approximately 6 ounces each), peeled and juiced
1½ cups verjus
1 fennel bulb, thinly sliced
1 shallot, thinly sliced
1 clove garlic, thinly sliced
2 whole star anise
1 tablespoon fennel seed
3 sprigs thyme

Horseradish Cream
1 quart heavy cream
1 fennel bulb, thinly sliced
2 cloves garlic, thinly sliced
3 shallots, thinly sliced
¼ cup prepared horseradish
Salt and white pepper

Toasted Cauliflower
1 large head of cauliflower
1 tablespoon butter
1 tablespoon grapeseed oil
Salt and white pepper

Salmon
8 6-ounce salmon fillets
Salt and pepper
2 tablespoons whole thyme leaves
¼ cup grapeseed oil, divided
½ cup crème fraîche
Lemon oil
2 tablespoons chive batons

Braised Pulled Suckling Pig
with Cinnamon Jus, Swiss Chard and Poached Quince Serves Twenty

This is the big daddy—the pièce de résistance of Restaurant Nicholas. If it were a song, it would be the encore. People go crazy for it! Some customers who have eaten at the restaurant more than 20 times have never had an entrée OTHER than the Braised Pulled Suckling Pig. When I took it off the menu a few years ago, upset diners wrote complaint letters. I would love to tell you that I've always envisioned the suckling pig to be our signature dish, but sometimes it's the customers who make that decision.

I first encountered suckling pig when I was the sommelier at Jean Georges in Manhattan. Occasionally, it would appear on the menu of Nougatine, the casual café adjacent to the main dining room. The pigs were roasted whole, then sliced to order. Every person got a different cut, depending whether their portion was sliced from the leg or the shoulder. The presentation wasn't the most elegant, but the flavor was truly amazing.

The pigs came from a small family-owned operation called Four Story Hill Farm in Pennsylvania. Their diet consisted solely of apples, which contributed to the meat's delicate flavor. The owners, a husband and wife, once came to the restaurant to taste how we prepared their pigs. I expected to see a sophisticated wealthy couple. Instead, both were clad in overalls and flannel—straight from the farm!

The couple seemed extremely excited for their meal. I remember telling them to compare how we cooked the pig to how they did it at home. You can imagine my surprise when they said that this was the first time they were going to taste one of their pigs. It took months to raise the animals and they couldn't afford to slaughter one for their own consumption. The genuine sincerity of these real farmers was inspiring. At that moment, I knew I would put suckling pig on the menu of my own restaurant someday.

When Restaurant Nicholas opened, we started testing out suckling pig recipes. I wanted the final product to be more consistent than the way it was prepared at Nougatine. It took more than three years and several attempts before we hit our mark. Today we go through four pigs a week, or 208 a year!

This recipe is not home friendly. We gave you the exact way we do it at the restaurant with a 25-pound suckling pig. Unless you have a professional-grade kitchen with a refrigerator big enough to hold the pig, an extra large roasting pan, and an oversized oven, this would be a potential train wreck. So we've also provided an alternate way to make this delicious dish with a pork shoulder and pig skins. While a bit easier to handle, it's no less time consuming—it will still take three days to complete.

INGREDIENTS

Pig Spice
30 black peppercorns
10 whole cloves
2 tablespoons coriander seed
5 whole star anise
5 bay leaves
2 tablespoons dried ginger powder
2½ tablespoons ground cinnamon
2 tablespoons ground nutmeg

Braised Pig
1 suckling pig (approximately
  25–30 pounds), split in half
1 celery root, rough chopped
2 onions, rough chopped
2 large carrots, rough chopped
2 parsnips, rough chopped
2 gallons Chicken Stock
  (see page 227)
2 cups apple cider vinegar
Grapeseed oil

PIG SPICE
Lightly toast the peppercorns, cloves, coriander seeds, star anise and bay leaves in a large sauté pan on medium heat for about 5 minutes. Allow to cool on a sheet tray. Grind the spices into a fine powder using a spice grinder. Mix in the remaining ground spices and reserve.

BRAISED PIG
Remove the pig's head and feet with a cleaver. Place the two halves skin-side down on a large sheet pan lined with parchment paper. Season the interior of each side with ¼ cup of Pig Spice. Place the head and feet in the seasoned cavity and wrap tightly with plastic wrap. Marinate in the refrigerator for 24 hours.

Preheat the oven to 350 degrees. Heat a large, heavy-bottomed pot on medium-high heat and coat the bottom with grapeseed oil. When the oil just begins to smoke, add the vegetables. Stir them frequently until they are darkly caramelized but not burned. Deglaze with apple cider vinegar and scrape up all the browned bits stuck to the bottom of the pot with a large wooden spoon. Add the stock and bring to a boil.

Divide the pig and place the halves into two roasting pans, skin-side down. Pour the boiling Chicken Stock and vegetables into the hotel pans. Fit a sheet of parchment paper over the tops of the hotel pans, tucking in any overhanging edges. Cover tightly with the lid or aluminum foil and roast for 5–6 hours. Cooking times will vary depending on the size of the pig. To check for doneness, remove the cover and poke at the hindquarter of the pig with a meat fork. If the meat releases easily from the bone, it is done.

Carefully remove the pans from the oven. Discard the parchment and let cool uncovered for 3½–4 hours.

When everything is cool enough to handle, strain the braising liquid through a chinois and discard the solids. Transfer 1 quart of the liquid to a pot and simmer until it reduces down to 1 cup. Reserve the remaining liquid.

continues »

Most butchers will be able to get pig skins. However, the shoulder can be braised and pulled, then served without the skin as a stylish alternative to traditional pulled pork.

To Pull the Pig

1 cup reduced braising liquid
Salt

Poached Quince

6 whole quince
2 quarts water
1 quart sugar
½ cup white wine vinegar
1 cinnamon stick

Swiss Chard

4 bunches Swiss chard
2 shallots, minced
2 tablespoons salt
1 tablespoon grapeseed oil

Parsnip Puree

20 large parsnips, peeled, cored,
    medium dice
1 pound butter, cubed
1½ cups milk, warm
¼ cup maple syrup
Pinch of freshly ground nutmeg
Salt
½ cup chives, finely chopped

TO PULL THE PIG

This is a long process. It is important to have plenty of room to work. Position one of the roasting pans with the pig in it directly in front of you. Have a large bowl nearby for the meat. Gently remove the rib cage, bone by bone. Along with the ribs there will be many small pieces of bone and cartilage. Remove and discard these.

Pull the meat from the pig and deposit it into the bowl. Take care not to include any small pieces of bone or cartilage. Be patient and continue to separate the meat from the rest of the carcass.

When the meat and bones have been removed, carefully roll up the skin like a carpet. Gently transfer the roll to a large sheet pan lined with parchment paper. Unroll the skin, being careful not to tear it.

Pick out any meat that may remain on the skin while it's on the sheet pan. Remove and discard as much fat from the skin as possible. Underneath a layer of fat on the top portion of the skin is the flank, a very thin and stringy piece of meat. Incorporate it with the rest of the pulled meat. Set aside the first cleaned skin and repeat the process with the other half.

Shred the meat with your hands or a fork. Season it liberally with salt. It can take ¼–½ cup of salt to properly season. Warm the reduced braising liquid and mix it into the meat.

Divide the meat between the 2 pieces of skin and spread it evenly in a layer 2–3 inches thick. Make sure you don't leave any gaps. Lay a piece of parchment paper over each side of pig and stack one sheet pan on top of the other. Place a third sheet pan on top of that and wrap the bundle very tightly with plastic wrap. Refrigerate for 24 hours.

PORTIONING

Remove the pig from the refrigerator and unwrap it. Invert each side onto a sheet pan or a cutting board so the skin side is facing up. Cut out portions from each piece using a 3½-inch ring mold. Collect the excess meat that remains on the skin and discard the leftover skin. Place each portion back into the ring mold, skin-side down, and pack the mold with the excess meat. Mold the portions so that each is a full, uniform disk.

Vacuum seal each portion in plastic. This pulls the meat together and helps it set into a more solid piece. This step can be omitted, however it does help prevent the meat from falling apart as it cooks. Refrigerate the vacuum-sealed portions until needed. This entire process can be done a few days in advance.

CINNAMON JUS

Bring the reserved braising liquid to a boil then lower the flame to medium low. Reduce the liquid to sauce consistency—until it's thick enough to coat the back of a spoon. Adjust the seasoning with salt.

POACHED QUINCE

Combine the water, sugar, vinegar and cinnamon in a large pot. Peel and quarter the quince, then remove the core from each quarter. Immediately transfer the pieces to the liquid to prevent them from oxidizing. Cover the floating quince with a clean kitchen towel.

Bring the liquid to a rolling boil for 10 seconds. Remove the pot from the heat and let it stand at room temperature for 90 minutes. When cool, store the quince in a plastic container with enough of the liquid to cover. Refrigerate until ready to use.

SWISS CHARD

Remove the leaves from the stalks of the Swiss chard. The leaves need to be washed multiple times in several changes of water until they are completely free of sand. Line a sheet tray with paper towels and lay the leaves on top to dry.

In a large pot, heat the oil over medium-high heat. Add the shallots then the chard. Season with salt and cook until wilted, stirring often. Drain the chard in a colander. Refrigerate until ready to use.

PARSNIP PUREE

Bring a large pot of salted water to a boil. Add the parsnips and cook until tender, about 10 minutes. Drain the parsnips in a colander.

Working in batches, place a quarter each of the parsnips, butter and milk in a blender. Begin blending on low and gradually increase the speed until the puree is smooth with no lumps. You may need to stop the blender and scrape down the sides several times to accomplish this. Transfer the puree to a bowl and continue with the remaining three batches. Stir in the maple syrup and nutmeg. Season with salt.

ASSEMBLY

Preheat the oven to 350 degrees. Heat a cast-iron pan until smoking. You may need several pans or work in batches depending on how many people you plan to serve. Coat the bottom of the pan with grapeseed oil and place the pig

portions in the pan, skin-side down. Transfer the pan to the oven and cook for 10 minutes until the meat is warmed through. Carefully turn the portions over with a spatula and allow them to rest in the hot pan for a minute or two.

Meanwhile, mound or twist ⅓ cup of the Swiss chard into a tight ball and place it on a sheet tray. Slice a piece of quince very thinly and fan it out on top the chard. Do this for however many people you are serving. Place the tray in the oven for 8–10 minutes. If needed, warm up the Parsnip Puree and the Cinnamon Jus on the stovetop.

To plate, place the pig portions, skin-side up, on each plate at six o'clock. The Swiss chard gets placed at eight o'clock and the Parsnip Puree at three o'clock. Sprinkle the chopped chives over the Parsnip Puree. Spoon the desired amount of sauce over the pig.

NOTES

SPECIAL EQUIPMENT: 2 large, deep roasting pans, chinois or fine-mesh strainer, coffee/spice grinder, 3½-inch ring mold, parchment paper, Cryovac or other vacuum-sealing machine, heavy cleaver, 3 large sheet pans.

 WINE PAIRING: This dish has so many layers of flavor that it needs a bold, fruity wine to stand up to the cinnamon and the quince. A Napa Valley Cabernet Sauvignon would be a wonderful match.

Braised Pulled Pork Shoulder with
Cinnamon Jus, Swiss Chard and Poached Quince Serves Eight

BRAISED PORK

Season the pork shoulder with the Pig Spice. Wrap in plastic wrap and marinate for 24 hours.

Preheat the oven to 350 degrees. Heat a large, heavy-bottomed pot on medium-high heat and coat the bottom with oil. When the oil just begins to smoke, add the vegetables. Stir them frequently until they're darkly caramelized but not burned. Deglaze with apple cider vinegar and scrape up all the browned bits left on the bottom of the pot with a large wooden spoon. Add the Chicken Stock and bring to a boil.

Place the pork shoulder in a deep braising pan. Pour the boiling Chicken Stock and vegetables into the pan. Cover and roast for 5–6 hours. To check for doneness, remove the cover and pierce the widest part of the pork with a meat fork. If the fork pierces through the meat with little to no resistance, it is done.

Carefully remove the pan from the oven. Let cool uncovered for 3½–4 hours.

Strain the braising liquid through a chinois and discard the solids. Transfer 1 quart of the liquid to a pot and simmer until it reduces down to 1 cup. Reserve the remaining liquid.

BRAISED PORK SKIN

Preheat the oven to 350 degrees. Place the pork skins in a large roasting pan. Bring the Chicken Stock to a boil in a separate pot, then pour it over the pork skins. Cover and cook for 2½ hours. Remove the pan from the oven and let it cool uncovered for at least 45 minutes. When it has cooled, drain and discard the liquid and reserve the skin.

Pull and shred the meat as you would for the whole suckling pig (see page 138). Spread the meat on the braised pork skin. If the skin is too big for the sheet tray you are using, you can cut it in half and use 2 trays. Place a sheet of parchment paper on top of the meat and then another sheet tray. Tightly wrap the trays together with plastic wrap and refrigerate overnight. Follow the remaining procedures for the suckling pig.

INGREDIENTS

Braised Pork

1 pork shoulder, boneless
   (approximately 8 pounds)
1 celery root, rough chopped
2 onions, rough chopped
2 large carrots, rough chopped
2 parsnips, rough chopped
2 gallons Chicken Stock
   (see page 227)
2 cups apple cider vinegar
Pig Spice (see page 136)
Grapeseed oil

Braised Pork Skin

1 pound pork skin
2 quarts Chicken Stock
   (see page 227)

Rack of Lamb with
Vegetable Bayaldi and Artichoke Gratin Serves Eight

INGREDIENTS

Bayaldi

2 white onions, thinly sliced
¼ cup thyme leaves
5 ripe plum tomatoes
3 yellow squash
3 zucchini
2 eggplant, quartered lengthwise
2 tablespoons grapeseed oil
Extra-virgin olive oil
Salt and black pepper

Artichoke Gratin

4 large artichokes
10 lemons, juiced
5 russet potatoes
1 quart heavy cream
Salt and black pepper

BAYALDI

Heat a heavy-bottomed pot over medium-low heat. Add the grapeseed oil. Gently sweat the onions until they are soft and translucent. Season with salt and pepper. Remove from heat and add the thyme leaves. Spread the onions out on a plate and cool in the refrigerator.

Slice the tomatoes, yellow squash and zucchini in half lengthwise. Slice the halves into approximately $1/8$-inch-thick half-moons. Trim the eggplant until it is similar in size to the other vegetables and slice in the same fashion.

Preheat the oven to 400 degrees. Spoon approximately 2 cups of the sweated onion into a large rectangle baking dish and spread out evenly. Layer the eggplant slices over the onion, overlapping each eggplant slice by about ½ inch. It should resemble ½-inch shingles. Follow the eggplant layer with a layer of zucchini, then layers of squash and tomato. Repeat until the entire dish is full. Gently press the Bayaldi down with your hand to set the slices in place. Generously coat the Bayaldi with extra-virgin olive oil and season with salt. Cover the baking dish with plastic wrap then aluminum foil. Bake for 45 minutes. Remove from the oven and let cool uncovered.

Note: The Bayaldi can be assembled and cooked 1 day ahead. When cool, cover and refrigerate until needed.

ARTICHOKE GRATIN

Preheat the oven to 375 degrees. Fill a large bowl with cold water and add the lemon juice. Remove the outer leaves from each artichoke. Cut off the top 2 inches of 1 artichoke and discard. Trim the sides and stem, leaving a smooth, pale yellow cylinder. With a spoon, remove the fibrous choke from the top of the cylinder. Submerge the cleaned artichoke into the lemon water to prevent it from oxidizing. Repeat the procedure for the remaining artichokes.

Pour the heavy cream in a large pot and bring it to a boil. Remove from heat and season with salt and pepper. The cream should remain hot when assembling the gratin.

Coat the bottom of a half hotel pan or large rectangular casserole dish (approximately 9 x 11 inches) with nonstick cooking spray. Line the pan with parchment paper and coat it with cooking spray. Coat the bottom with a thin layer of heavy cream.

Peel the potatoes and submerge them in cold water to prevent oxidization. Using a mandoline, slice a potato lengthwise into thin ovals and layer the slices into the hotel pan, overlapping each slice by approximately ½ inch. Be sure the slices are layered in the same direction.

After the first layer is complete, brush the potatoes with heavy cream and season lightly with salt and pepper. Repeat the layering process with the second layer perpendicular to the first layer.

continues »

The Bayaldi and the Artichoke Gratin are both time consuming. Each can be prepared a day ahead. Both are quite versatile and will suit many dishes. The artichoke can be omitted from the gratin, if desired.

For the third layer, thinly slice 2 artichokes lengthwise and layer them atop the potatoes. The artichoke slices do not need to be layered uniformly. Brush with cream and season.

Continue layering potatoes and artichokes until the pan is ¾ full. Pour the remaining cream over the top and cover with foil. Place the hotel pan on a baking sheet to catch any spills and bake for 1 hour and 20 minutes.

When the time has elapsed, remove the foil and bake for an additional 30 minutes.

To check for doneness, pierce the gratin with a paring knife. If the blade goes through with no resistance, the gratin is done. Remove from the oven and let cool at room temperature for 1 hour. Refrigerate for at least 6 hours to set completely.

To portion the gratin, invert the pan onto a cutting board. Carefully remove the pan and parchment paper. With a long serrated knife, trim the ends to leave a perfect rectangle. The gratin can either be cut into 3-inch-by-3-inch squares or punched out using a ring mold. The individual portions can be wrapped in plastic and refrigerated for up to 3 days.

ASSEMBLY

Preheat the oven to 400 degrees. Season the lamb racks with salt and pepper. Heat a large cast-iron skillet or oven-safe sauté pan on medium heat. Coat the bottom with grapeseed oil. When the oil is hot, sear the lamb on all sides for approximately 3 minutes per side. Transfer the lamb to a baking pan lined with a rack and roast until medium rare, about 15 minutes or until the lamb's internal temperature is 130 degrees.

Meanwhile, place the Bayaldi in the oven and bake for 15 minutes or until heated through. Place the gratin portions on a sheet pan lined with parchment paper and bake them for 10–15 minutes or until hot.

When the lamb has finished cooking, remove the racks from the pan and allow them to rest at room temperature for 5 minutes. Allow the Bayaldi to cool for 5 minutes before cutting it into 3-inch-by-3-inch squares, similar to the portions of gratin.

Using a sharp knife, remove the first lamb chop from the rack. This piece will accent the dish and add an elegant dimension to the final plate, however it can be omitted if you prefer. Carefully slice the rack of bones away from the meat, cutting as close to the bone as possible so as not to lose too much meat. Slice the meat into 4 or 5 medallions.

To plate, shingle the sliced lamb across the plate. Place the gratin and the Bayaldi opposite from each other. Pour desired amount of sauce atop the lamb and garnish the sauce with fresh picked thyme.

NOTES
SPECIAL EQUIPMENT: Mandoline.

 WINE PAIRING: Red Bordeaux and lamb are one of my favorite flavor combinations. Try something from the Pauillac region. Predominately Cabernet Sauvignon, Pauillac will have enough intensity to stand up to the full flavor of lamb.

Lamb
4 lamb racks, cleaned
Salt and black pepper
Grapeseed oil
Thyme, picked
Lamb Sauce (see page 232)

The Duck Confit adds a nice crunchy texture to this dish, though it can be omitted.

Roasted Duck Breast with Corn Soufflé and Date Puree Serves Eight

If you choose not to make the confit, you can purchase individual duck breasts instead of whole birds. Any extra confit can be frozen in duck fat for several months.

DATE PUREE

Place the dates in a large bowl. Bring a pot of water to a boil and pour it over the dates to cover. Let steep for 10 minutes to soften. Remove the skins and pits from each date. Puree the dates and lemon juice in a food processor until smooth. Pass the puree through a tamis. Reserve.

DUCK GLAZE

Whisk the ingredients together in a small bowl and reserve.

CORN SOUFFLÉ

Preheat oven to 400 degrees. Reserve ⅓ cup of the corn and set aside. Combine cream, milk, eggs, remaining corn and salt in a bowl and blend with the immersion blender. Slowly incorporate the flour and blend thoroughly. Fold in the reserved corn. Refrigerate until needed.

Spray the inside of each ramekin with nonstick cooking spray and fill it ¾ of the way with batter. Any extra batter can be refrigerated for another use. Transfer ramekins to a sheet tray and bake until the cakes rise, about 7 minutes. When the soufflés are out of the oven, they will slightly deflate. Let the soufflés cool momentarily before removing them from the ramekins.

DUCK CONFIT

Heat a sauté pan on medium-high heat and add the grapeseed oil. When the oil is smoking hot, add the confit. Work in batches so you don't overcrowd the pan. Saute until the meat becomes crispy. Reserve.

ASSEMBLY

Preheat oven to 400 degrees. Trim any excess skin around the edges of the breasts. With a sharp knife, score a crosshatch pattern about ¼ inch deep into the skin.

Lay the breasts, skin-side down, in a dry, hot sauté pan over medium heat. After about 3 minutes, the skin will begin to render off fat. Lower the temperature to medium-low. Continue cooking until the skin is golden brown and most of the fat has been rendered. Occasionally, baste the meat with the rendered duck fat.

Transfer the breasts, skin-side up, to a sheet pan lined with a rack. Rub the glaze over the skin and roast until they have reached a temperature of medium rare, about 6 minutes. Remove from the oven and let the breasts rest for 5 minutes. Rub another coat of glaze on the skin.

Warm the corn soufflés in the oven if they had cooled off.

Lay the breasts on a cutting board, skin-side down, and slice into thin pieces. Place a corn soufflé in the center of a plate and shingle the sliced duck around it. Top the cake with duck confit. Spoon desired amount of sauce atop the breast.

NOTES

SPECIAL EQUIPMENT: Immersion blender, tamis, 8 3-inch ramekins.

 WINE PAIRING: Crozes-Hermitage, a village in the Northern Rhone Valley, is one of my favorite sources for aromatic, lush Syrah. Its pristine, fresh fruit is just perfect with the date puree.

INGREDIENTS

Date Puree
1 pound whole dates
1 lemon, juiced

Duck Glaze
½ teaspoon Confit Spice
  (see page 228)
⅓ cup honey
½ tablespoon rice wine vinegar

Corn Soufflés
3 ears of corn, kernels removed
  from cob
2 cups all-purpose flour
1 quart heavy cream
5 eggs
5 egg yolks
2 tablespoons milk
1½ teaspoons salt

Duck Confit
2 cups Duck Confit (see page 228)
2 tablespoons grapeseed oil

Duck Breast
8 duck breasts (approximately 6
  ounces each)
1 cup Duck Sauce (see page 229)

New York Strip Steak, Scallion-Potato Cake, Oven-Dried Tomatoes and Roasted Portobello Mushrooms Serves Eight

INGREDIENTS

Scallion-Potato Cake
3 large russet potatoes
1 cup sour cream
1 bunch scallions, thinly sliced
1 tablespoon salt
White pepper
8 tablespoons grapeseed oil
½ cup Wondra flour

Portobello Mushrooms
2 large or 4 medium portobello
 mushrooms, cleaned and stems
 removed
4 cloves garlic, crushed
4 sprigs thyme
1 cup grapeseed oil
1 tablespoon salt
Black pepper

Oven-dried Tomatoes
4 ripe Roma tomatoes
2 cloves garlic, minced
10 sprigs thyme, leaves picked
 and finely chopped
1 cup extra-virgin olive oil
Pinch of salt
Pinch of sugar

Bone-Marrow-Horseradish Butter
1 pound butter, room
 temperature
1 cup prepared horseradish,
 drained
3 pieces marrow bones
3 tablespoons salt

SCALLION-POTATO CAKE
Preheat the oven to 500 degrees. Roast the potatoes for 1 hour or until a paring knife can pass easily through their centers. Let the potatoes cool for 5–10 minutes.

Cut the potatoes in half lengthwise. Position a cooling rack over a large bowl. With the skin side facing up, push the potato halves through the rack. Discard the skins. Combine potatoes, sour cream, scallions, salt and pepper, and let cool completely.

Line a baking sheet with parchment paper. With the ring mold on the parchment, fill it with the potato mixture and carefully remove the mold. Repeat with the other 7 cakes. Refrigerate for 20 minutes, or up to 2 days, to allow the potatoes to stiffen further.

To cook, heat 1 tablespoon of oil in a sauté pan on medium-high heat. Dredge each side of the cake in flour. Cook for 2 minutes on each side. Warm through in a hot oven when ready to serve.

PORTOBELLO MUSHROOMS
Preheat oven to 350 degrees. With a paring knife, peel the top layer of skin off each mushroom. Using a spoon, scrape off the dark gills. Line a baking sheet with parchment paper. Place the mushrooms onto the baking sheet with the concave part facing up. Saturate each mushroom with the grapeseed oil. Place the thyme and garlic on top and roast for 2 hours.

Remove the garlic and thyme and let the mushrooms cool. Cut the mushroom on a bias to yield about 5 or 6 slices per mushroom.

OVEN-DRIED TOMATOES
Bring a large pot of salted water to a boil. Remove the stem end and score an "X" in the other end of each tomato. Have a large bowl of ice water ready. Submerge the tomatoes in the boiling water for 15–30 seconds or until the skin starts to peel away from the "X." Immediately transfer to the ice bath. When cool, remove the skins. Stand the tomatoes on their end and quarter lengthwise. Remove the seeds from each quarter and place the fillets on a towel to dry.

Preheat oven to 250 degrees. Place the tomato quarters, skin-side down, on a sheet tray lined with parchment paper. Whisk the olive oil, salt, sugar, garlic and thyme in a bowl. Spoon the mixture over the tomato wedges and roast for 3 hours. The tomatoes should be wilted and most of the moisture evaporated. Lay the tomatoes on paper towels to remove any excess moisture and oil. They can be made ahead and refrigerated for up to 3 days. Warm them through in the oven before serving.

BONE-MARROW-HORSERADISH BUTTER
Soak the bone marrow in water for at least 24 hours in the refrigerator. Remove it from the water and bring to room temperature. Scoop out the marrow with the back of a spoon. Be careful since the bones can be sharp. Three bones should yield about 1 cup of marrow. Pass the marrow through a tamis with a rubber spatula.

continues »

The Bone-Marrow-Horseradish Butter
is not the easiest to prepare, however it
transforms this dish from a normal meat-
and-potatoes dinner to an extraordinary
entrée worthy of a fine steakhouse.

Transfer the marrow, butter, horseradish and salt to a food processor. Incorporate thoroughly. This recipe yields more than you will need. The remaining butter can be frozen for another application.

NEW YORK STRIP STEAKS

Preheat oven to 450 degrees. Season each steak generously with salt and pepper. Heat a large sauté pan or cast-iron skillet on high heat with enough grapeseed oil to coat the bottom of the pan. When the oil is nearly smoking, add the steaks. This can either be done in batches or with several pans. Cook for 2 minutes on one side then turn them over. Add 1 tablespoon of butter for each steak and baste with a large spoon. Cook for an additional 2 minutes. Transfer the pans to the oven and finish cooking the steaks to desired doneness, approximately 3 minutes for medium rare. Remove steaks from pan and allow to rest for 5 minutes. These steaks can also be grilled, if you prefer.

WILTED SPINACH

Heat the grapeseed oil on high heat in a pot large enough to fit all the spinach. When the oil is hot, add the spinach. Toss with a spoon and season with salt and pepper. When the spinach is just wilted, transfer to a colander to remove any excess moisture. The spinach will continue to wilt in the colander.

ASSEMBLY

Slice the steak against the grain and shingle the pieces along the bottom half of the plate. Spoon 2 tablespoons of the marrow butter on top of the meat. Sprinkle with coarse salt, if desired. Mound ½ cup of spinach on the top half of the plate. Top the spinach with 2 slices each of the mushrooms and tomatoes. Place the potato cake next to the spinach.

NOTES

SPECIAL EQUIPMENT: 3-inch ring mold, tamis.

 WINE PAIRING: Steak dinners are the reason why Napa Valley Cabernet Sauvignon is so popular in America. The fruitiness of a Cabernet Sauvignon from this region is the perfect foil for the richness of a great steak.

New York Strip Steaks

8 New York strip steaks, 8
 ounces each
8 tablespoons grapeseed oil,
 divided
8 tablespoons butter, divided
Salt and pepper

Wilted Spinach

3 1-pound bags
 pre-washed spinach
1 tablespoon grapeseed oil
Salt and white pepper

Veal with Scallion Whipped Potatoes, White Asparagus and Trumpet Royale Mushrooms Serves Eight

SCALLION WHIPPED POTATOES

Place the scallions and grapeseed oil in a blender and puree until smooth. Refrigerate and reserve.

Fill a large pot with cold water, season liberally with salt, and add the potatoes. Bring to a boil then reduce the heat to a simmer. Cook the potatoes approximately 25–30 minutes until they are tender. Potatoes are done if there is no resistance when pierced with a paring knife.

Drain the potatoes and allow them to cool slightly. Hold each potato in your hand with a kitchen towel and remove the skin with a paring knife. Grind the peeled potatoes and butter in a food mill. Place a fine-mesh tamis over a bowl and push the potatoes through using a rubber spatula. Incorporate the milk and adjust the seasoning with salt and pepper. If the potatoes are stiff, add more butter and milk until the desired consistency is reached. Keep potatoes warm until ready to serve.

ASSEMBLY

Have your butcher cut a veal loin into 8-ounce portions. Tie each portion with 2 pieces of butcher's twine to maintain a consistent shape while cooking.

Bring a large pot of salted water to a boil. With a vegetable peeler, remove the outer layer of skin from each asparagus stalk. Blanch the asparagus for 1 minute then immediately shock the stalks in a large ice bath to stop the cooking process. When the asparagus is completely cooled, remove it from the ice water and allow it to dry. Trim approximately 2–3 inches off the bottom end and discard. Cut the asparagus into 1½-inch pieces and reserve.

With a paring knife, remove the caps from each mushroom. Peel the outer layer of skin from each stem and slice off the bottoms. Cut the caps and stems into a medium dice and reserve.

Preheat the oven to 450 degrees. Season each portion of veal with salt and pepper. Heat a large sauté pan on medium-high heat. When the pan is hot, coat the bottom with grapeseed oil. Sear the veal for about 4 minutes on each side. Do this in batches so you don't overcrowd the pan.

Transfer the seared veal to a baking rack on a sheet pan and roast for 6–8 minutes for medium. Remove the veal from the oven and let it rest for 5 minutes.

While the meat is resting, heat 1 tablespoon of grapeseed oil in a sauté pan on medium heat. Add the mushrooms and season with salt. Sauté for 1 minute then add the asparagus and butter. Cook for an additional minute to warm the asparagus through. Adjust the seasoning with salt and pepper.

Stir ⅓ cup of scallion puree into the whipped potatoes. Heat over medium-low heat, stirring frequently until hot.

Remove the strings from the veal and slice each piece against the grain into thirds. Place on the plate along with the scallion potatoes, mushrooms and asparagus. Spoon desired amount of warm veal sauce on top of each portion.

NOTES

SPECIAL EQUIPMENT: Food mill, fine-mesh tamis, butcher's twine.

 WINE PAIRING: This loin of veal has delicate flavors. I think the perfect pairing would be an elegant Pinot Noir from the Côte de Beaune in Burgundy. Select a Volnay or Pommard.

INGREDIENTS

1 bunch white asparagus
8 ounces trumpet
   royale mushrooms
8 portions tied veal loins (approximately 8 ounces each)
1 cup Veal Sauce (see page 232)
1 tablespoon butter
2 tablespoons grapeseed oil
Salt and pepper

Scallion Whipped Potatoes

4–5 large russet potatoes, skin on
8 ounces butter (2 sticks), cubed
⅓ cup milk, warm
2 bunches scallions,
   green parts only
¼ cup grapeseed oil
Salt and pepper

Roasted Organic Chicken Serves Eight

Looking back, I often realize how naïve I was as a young chef. At the inception of Restaurant Nicholas, I intentionally didn't have chicken on the menu. Despite this omission, we would get a table of eight diners, for example, and all would order the tasting menu except for one person. "Can I just get a chicken?" they almost always asked. It happened at least once a week.

To appease this person, I created a chicken entrée. A boned-out chicken leg was stuffed with sweetbreads and foie gras, rolled up, seared, roasted and sliced. It was fantastic. In fact, it was mentioned in our first four-star review. The press loved it. My loyal customers loved it. The one person for whom I created it, however, did not. I threw my hands up in the air. I was deflated.

I now realize my rookie mistake. Sometimes someone just wants chicken. No truffles, no caviar, no foie gras… just chicken.

It's been often said that you can test a chef's mettle by how well he can cook chicken. I took that seriously when creating this chicken entrée, which, incidentally, is now the most popular item in our lounge. If there was going to be a basic roasted chicken dish on the menu at Restaurant Nicholas, every component had to be perfect.

It didn't surprise me that when this dish first hit the menu, we only sold a handful each week. After all, it was just chicken. However, everyone who ordered it agreed that it was the best chicken they had ever eaten. While the ingredients are pretty ordinary—mashed potatoes and some baby vegetables—the secret is in the technique.

The breast is brined for 24 hours then air-dried for another 24 hours. The brine makes the breast extremely moist while the drying helps the skin become beautifully crisp.

INGREDIENTS

Chicken Brine

8 bone-in organic chicken
  breasts
1 gallon water
½ cup salt

Chicken Confit

8 chicken thighs
Confit Method (see Duck Confit
  on page 228)

Whipped Potatoes

8 Yukon Gold potatoes
12 ounces butter, cubed
1 cup milk, warm
Salt and white pepper

CHICKEN BRINE
Combine the salt and water, and soak the chicken in the brine for 24 hours. Remove the chicken and pat dry. Allow the chicken to air dry on a sheet tray lined with a rack in the refrigerator for another 24 hours.

CHICKEN CONFIT
For this application, the skin is to remain intact on the thigh.

WHIPPED POTATOES
Place the potatoes in a large pot and cover with cold water. Season the water with salt. Bring the water to a boil then lower to a simmer. Cook the potatoes until they are tender, approximately 1 hour.

Remove the skin from each potato with a paring knife. Quarter or slice the peeled potatoes and run them through a food mill along with the butter. With a rubber spatula, pass the potatoes through a tamis into a large bowl. Whisk in the milk. The whipped potatoes should be loose but not runny. Adjust the seasoning with salt and pepper.

BABY VEGETABLES
Bring a large pot of salted water to a boil. Blanch each vegetable separately until tender then immediately shock in an ice bath. Drain on paper towels and reserve. To finish, warm the vegetables, butter and water in a medium saucepot. The butter will emulsify with the water and coat the vegetables in a light butter glaze. Season with salt and pepper.

continues »

As simple as it is, this dish is very time consuming. Start to finish, you will need three days. The confit thighs are not essential to the dish, although they are my favorite part. The sauce can be made in advance and used for other chicken, veal or pheasant dishes.

BROWN CHICKEN SAUCE (YIELDS 1 QUART)

Preheat the oven to 450 degrees. Place the chicken bones on a sheet pan lined with a rack and roast for 45 minutes or until well browned. Remove the bones from the pan and set aside. Be careful. The chicken bones will render a lot of fat.

Heat a large, heavy-bottomed pot over medium-high heat. Coat the bottom with grapeseed oil. When the oil is hot, add the carrots, onions, celery root and garlic. Cook until the vegetables are caramelized, about 10 minutes. Add the tomatoes and the tomato paste, and cook until the tomatoes break down and begin to stick to the bottom of the pot, approximately 10 minutes. Deglaze with the sherry, scraping up the brown bits that have stuck to the bottom of the pan.

Add the stock and browned chicken bones to the pot and bring to a boil. Reduce heat to the lowest simmer and slowly cook for 2 hours. Periodically skim the surface with a ladle to remove any impurities.

Strain the sauce through a chinois or fine-mesh strainer and discard the solids. Continue reducing the sauce until approximately a quart remains. Adjust the seasoning with salt. With the heat off, steep thyme sprigs in the sauce for 30 minutes. Strain the sauce one last time and reserve.

ASSEMBLY

Preheat oven to 425 degrees. Heat a sauté pan over medium heat and coat the bottom with grapeseed oil. When the oil is hot, sear the chicken breasts, skin-side down, for 5–7 minutes until the skin is brown and crispy. You'll probably have to use 2 or 3 pans so as not to crowd the pan and inhibit browning. Turn the breasts again so that the skin is down and roast in the oven for 15 minutes. Turn the breasts skin-side up and roast an additional 10 minutes. Allow the chicken to rest on a cooling rack for approximately 8 minutes.

While the breasts are resting, heat a sauté pan on medium heat and coat the bottom with grapeseed oil. Place the thighs in the very hot oil, skin-side down, and transfer the pan to the oven. Roast for 8 minutes. When the skin is golden brown and crispy, remove the pan from the oven and turn the thighs over so that the skin is up. Allow them to rest in the hot pan for 2 minutes, then remove and reserve.

Transfer the chicken breasts to a cutting board. Slide a sharp knife between the breast meat and the rib cage to remove the bones. Remove the wishbone if that is still intact.

Slice the breast on the bias into 4 pieces.

To complete, fan the breast on the bottom portion of a plate. Spoon the vegetables and potatoes on the top portion of the plate. Lean the crispy confit thigh against the vegetables. Pour desired amount of chicken sauce over the breast.

NOTES

SPECIAL EQUIPMENT: Food mill, fine-mesh tamis, chinois or fine-mesh strainer.

WINE PAIRING: This Sunday-night classic is best with a fruity, generous wine. Choose a Grenache-based Cotes du Rhone. It's a great match.

Baby Vegetables

1 bunch baby carrots, peeled and
  cut into pieces similar in size to
  the turnips and squash
1 bunch baby turnips, peeled and
  quartered
16 pattypan squash, quartered
4 tablespoons butter
1 tablespoon water
Salt and pepper

Brown Chicken Sauce

1 carrot, rough chopped
1 onion, rough chopped
½ celery root, rough chopped
½ head garlic, skin intact and split
¼ cup tomato paste
1 cup dry sherry
4 tomatoes, quartered
3 quarts Chicken Stock
  (see page 227)
Grapeseed oil
2 chicken carcasses,
  cut into pieces
8–10 sprigs thyme

Braised Short Ribs with Tamarind Sauce Serves Eight

SPICE MIX

Place the Szechuan peppercorns, allspice, bay leaves, coriander seeds, cloves and cumin into a medium-sized sauté pan. Heat the sauté pan over low flame until the spices become slightly toasted and aromatic. Transfer them to a spice grinder along with the white and black peppercorns. Pulse into a fine powder. Combine with the ground cinnamon and cayenne pepper.

PICKLED MANGO AND PAPAYA

Peel the fruit and slice them into thin pieces. In a medium bowl, toss the mango slices with 2 teaspoons of Spice Mix. In a separate bowl, repeat the process with the papaya.

Combine the vinegar and sugar in a saucepot. When the liquid reaches a boil, add the lemon zest. Divide the pickling liquid among the two bowls of fruit. Allow them to cool to room temperature then refrigerate until needed.

SHORT RIBS

Combine the first 9 ingredients in a blender and puree until smooth. This will be the braising liquid.

Preheat the oven to 350 degrees. Liberally season each short rib with salt, pepper and the remaining spice mix.

Heat a Dutch oven or large braising pan over medium-high heat. When the pan is hot, coat the bottom with grapeseed oil. Sear the short ribs on all sides until nicely browned.

Meanwhile, bring the braising liquid to a boil.

Transfer the short ribs to a sheet tray lined with a few paper towels. Discard any excess oil left in the pan. Return the short ribs to the pan. Pour the braising liquid over the short ribs, cover, and place in the oven. Cook until the short ribs are tender, about 2½–3 hours.

Place the short ribs in the refrigerator to cool. The fat will eventually rise to the surface and solidify. Remove it with a spoon and discard.

Carefully remove the bones from the short ribs and trim off any large pieces of fat that may still be attached to the meat.

SAUCE

Pour the braising liquid into a saucepot. Bring it to a boil then reduce to a simmer. Add 1 cup of the Pickled Papaya. Using an immersion blender, puree the papaya into the sauce. Adjust the seasoning with salt and pepper.

HORSERADISH WHIPPED POTATOES

Place potatoes in a large pot and cover them with cold water. Season the water with salt. Bring it to a boil then lower the heat and simmer for approximately 1 hour or until the potatoes are tender.

Remove the skin from each potato with a paring knife. Run the potatoes and the cubed butter through a food mill. With a rubber spatula, pass the potatoes through a tamis into a large bowl. Fold in the milk. The whipped potatoes should be loose but not runny. Stir in the horseradish. Adjust the seasoning with salt and pepper.

ASSEMBLY

Combine the short ribs and sauce on the stovetop and heat on medium until warmed through.

Spoon the whipped potatoes into the center of a shallow bowl. Place the short ribs atop the potatoes. Garnish with the chopped herbs and desired amount of sauce.

NOTES

SPECIAL EQUIPMENT: Dutch oven (optional), electric coffee/spice grinder, immersion blender, food mill, fine-mesh tamis.

 WINE PAIRING: A bold American Syrah has enough jammy fruit notes and spicy characteristics to stand up to the layers of different flavors in this dish.

INGREDIENTS

Spice Mix
½ teaspoon black pepper
½ teaspoon white pepper
1 tablespoon Szechuan peppercorns
½ tablespoon allspice
2 bay leaves
1½ teaspoons coriander seeds
½ teaspoon cloves
1 tablespoon cumin
½ tablespoon ground cinnamon
1 teaspoon cayenne pepper
1 teaspoon sea salt

Pickled Mango and Papaya
2 ripe mangos
2 ripe papayas
4 cups white distilled vinegar
2 cup sugar
4 teaspoons Spice Mix, divided
Zest of 1 lemon

Short Ribs
4 cups water
¼ cup pickled mangos
1¼ cup ginger, chopped
1 clove garlic
½ cup dark brown sugar
¼ cup Worcestershire sauce
1 cup tamarind paste
3 tablespoons Spice Mixture
4 tablespoons tomato paste
8 pounds beef short ribs, trimmed
½ cup water
Coarse salt and black pepper
Grapeseed oil

Horseradish Whipped Potatoes
8 Yukon Gold potatoes, skin intact
6 ounces butter, cubed
1 cup milk, warm
¼ cup prepared horseradish
Salt and white pepper
Tarragon and parsley, finely chopped for garnish

Filet Mignon Poached in
Red Wine with Potato-Mushroom Rosti Serves Four

INGREDIENTS

Potato-Mushroom Rosti

3 large russet potatoes

2 egg yolks

2 cups mushrooms (any variety),
   medium dice

1 shallot, minced

¼ cup carrots, brunoise

3 cloves garlic, minced

1 tablespoon thyme, chopped

¼ cup cream sherry

¼ cup sherry vinegar

¼ cup Parmesan cheese, grated

Grapeseed oil

Nonstick cooking spray

Salt and pepper

Filet Mignon

4 filet mignons (approximately 8
   ounces each), tied

1 bottle full-flavored red wine,
   like Syrah

1 teaspoon cloves

2 tablespoons black peppercorns

1 tablespoon coriander seed

4 whole star anise

POTATO-MUSHROOM ROSTI

Preheat the oven to 350 degrees. Heat a large, oven-safe sauté pan on medium heat. Coat the bottom with grapeseed oil. Add the mushrooms and shallot and sauté for about 5 minutes. Add the garlic and carrots. Season with salt and pepper. Continue to cook until most of the liquid has cooked out of the mushrooms.

Deglaze the pan with the sherry and sherry vinegar, stirring to loosen anything that has stuck to the bottom of the pan. When most of the liquid has evaporated, about 2 minutes, remove the pan from the heat and add the thyme. Adjust the seasoning with salt and set aside.

Wash and peel the potatoes. Using the mandoline with the fine julienne blade, grate the potatoes into a large bowl. Add the egg yolks and Parmesan and season with salt and pepper. Mix thoroughly.

Heat a large sauté pan on medium heat. Coat the bottom with nonstick cooking spray. Spread half the potatoes into the sauté pan. Spread the mushroom mixture on top of the potatoes then spread the remaining potatoes over the mushrooms. Smooth out the top with a spoon or spatula. Transfer the pan to the oven and bake for 8 minutes.

Remove the pan from the oven and carefully flip the rosti over onto a sheet tray. Return it to the oven and bake for an additional 8 minutes. Allow it to cool slightly before cutting it into wedges to serve.

FILET MIGNON

Place the spices in a coffee filter and tie with butcher's twine to create a sachet. Add the wine and sachet to a heavy-bottomed pot and bring it 170 degrees. Submerge the filets in the wine and poach for 8–10 minutes for medium rare. Cook an additional 4–5 minutes for medium.

Remove the filets from the liquid and allow them to rest on a sheet tray lined with a rack for 5 minutes. Remove the strings and slice horizontally.

Note: This technique does not translate well for steaks cooked over the temperature of medium.

Serve the filet mignons with Veal Sauce (page 232) and Onion Fettuccini (page 176).

NOTES

SPECIAL EQUIPMENT: Coffee filter, butcher's twine, instant–read thermometer, mandoline with fine julienne blade.

 WINE PAIRING: Since the filet was poached in a Syrah or similar fruity varietal, use that same style of wine to drink. A radically different style of red wine could create conflicting flavors on your palate.

Moroccan Braised Lamb Shank Serves Eight

INGREDIENTS

8 lamb shanks
4 shallots, minced
6 cloves garlic, minced
2 tablespoons ginger, minced
1 stick cinnamon
1 tablespoon coriander seed
½ tablespoon red pepper flakes
1 tablespoon green cardamom
1 tablespoon lavender
1 tablespoon whole cloves
1 tablespoon shaved nutmeg
5 whole star anise
1 cup honey
1 cup rice wine vinegar
1 cup lemon juice
1 cup soy sauce
1 cup plum tomato puree
1 cup tomato paste
½ cup chopped cilantro
2–3 quarts Chicken Stock
   (see page 227)
Salt and pepper
Grapeseed oil

Liberally season each lamb shank with salt and pepper. Heat a large, heavy-bottomed pot over medium-high heat. Coat the bottom with grapeseed oil. When the oil is hot, carefully add the lamb shanks. Do not overcrowd the pot. Cook in batches, if necessary. Sear on one side until caramelized to a golden brown, about 5–8 minutes. Turn the shanks over and repeat. Transfer the seared shanks to a sheet tray to rest.

Preheat the oven to 325 degrees. Combine the cinnamon, coriander seed, red pepper flakes, cardamom, lavender, cloves, nutmeg and star anise in a dry sauté pan. Toast over medium heat, tossing often, until the spices are lightly browned and the seeds begin to pop. Remove from heat and let cool. Finely grind the toasted spices in a spice grinder and set aside.

Heat a large braising pot or Dutch oven over low heat. Add about 2 tablespoons of grapeseed oil. Sweat the shallots, ginger and garlic for 5 minutes, stirring occasionally. You don't want any caramelization on the shallots. Add the honey, raise the heat to medium, and cook for 5 more minutes. Add the tomato paste and ground spices and cook for an additional 5 minutes, constantly stirring. Finally add the vinegar, lemon juice, soy sauce, tomato puree, Chicken Stock and cilantro. Transfer the seared lamb shanks to the pot. The lamb should be covered in liquid. If not, add more Chicken Stock. Bring the liquid to a boil, cover and place in the oven. Cook for 3½ hours.

To check for doneness, pierce the widest part of the shank with a paring knife. If the meat releases from the bone with no resistance, it is done.

Remove the pot from the oven. Using a ladle, remove and discard as much of the fat that has risen to the top as possible.

Note: Once cooled, the braised lamb shanks can be refrigerated for up to 3 days.

The braising liquid will act as the sauce for this dish, though you may need to adjust the seasoning with salt. Serve the shanks in a large bowl with couscous, steamed carrots, chopped cilantro and the desired amount of sauce.

NOTES
SPECIAL EQUIPMENT: Electric spice/coffee grinder, Dutch oven (optional).

 WINE PAIRING: Due to the complexity of this dish, a full-bodied wine is needed to stand up to the varying layers of spice. Try a Ribera del Duero from Spain. The fruity nature of Ribera del Duero, made from the Tempranillo grape, is strong but won't overpower the spices.

Dealing with a bone-in leg of lamb can be somewhat difficult. A boned, rolled and tied leg of lamb can be substituted. For an additional side keeping with the Middle Eastern theme, try couscous.

Roasted Leg of Lamb with Hummus and Cucumber Salad Serves Eight

Leg of lamb is one of the few red meats that is better cooked to a temperature of medium or higher. Any less and the meat will be a little tough. When cooking large roasts, I like to use a probe thermometer to alleviate the guesswork on the cooking time.

LAMB

Preheat the oven to 450 degrees. Position the rack in the center of the oven.

Rub the lamb with the garlic cloves. Combine the olive oil, salt and pepper and rub that into the lamb as well.

In a large bowl, toss the onions, carrots and celery root with a few drizzles of grapeseed oil. Add them to a large roasting pan. Place the lamb atop the vegetables, smooth side facing up. Insert a probe thermometer into the widest part of the leg.

Roast for 30 minutes at 450 degrees then lower the oven temperature to 325 degrees. Continue cooking until the internal temperature of the lamb reaches 135 degrees for medium, approximately 2–2½ hours.

Remove the lamb from the oven and allow it to rest at room temperature for at least 20 minutes.

CUCUMBER SALAD

Combine the yogurt, lemon juice, mint, Garlic Confit, Garlic Confit oil and olive oil. Mix thoroughly and season with salt. Dress the cucumbers with approximately ½ cup of the yogurt sauce. The remaining yogurt can be reserved as a sauce for the lamb.

HUMMUS

Toast the cumin in a small sauté pan over medium heat for approximately 1 minute, stirring frequently until fragrant.

Transfer the cumin to a blender. Add the rest of the ingredients and puree until smooth. Season with salt and pepper. For a smoother hummus, push it through a tamis or fine-mesh strainer after pureeing.

ASSEMBLY

Slicing a bone-in leg of lamb can be challenging. Begin by slicing the rounder part of the leg parallel to the bone. Grasp the bone with a kitchen towel to hold it steady. Rotate the leg and then slice the thinner, flatter side.

Serve the sliced lamb with the cucumber salad and hummus.

NOTES

SPECIAL EQUIPMENT: Probe thermometer.

 WINE PAIRING: The spicy, full-blown fruitiness of an Australian Shiraz has enough intensity to match the gaminess of the lamb.

INGREDIENTS

Lamb

1 bone-in leg of lamb, trimmed of fat (approximately 8 pounds)
⅓ cup cracked black peppercorns
⅓ cup salt
½ cup olive oil
4 cloves garlic, halved
3 carrots, rough chopped
2 onions, rough chopped
1 celery root, rough chopped
Grapeseed oil

Cucumber Salad

8 cucumbers, peeled, seeded and thinly sliced
2 cups plain yogurt
2 lemons, juiced
¼ cup mint, chopped
2 cloves Garlic Confit, minced (see page 229)
2 tablespoons Garlic Confit oil
¼ cup extra-virgin olive oil
Salt

Hummus

2 19-ounce cans chickpeas, drained and rinsed
2 cloves Garlic Confit (see page 229)
3 tablespoons Garlic Confit oil
2 tablespoons tahini paste
2 lemons, juiced
½ cup extra-virgin olive oil
1 tablespoon ground cumin
Salt and black pepper

Sous Vide Turkey Breast Serves Six

INGREDIENTS

1 turkey breast (approximately 3
   pounds), skin removed
1 gallon cold water
½ cup salt
½ cup buttermilk
5 sprigs thyme
2 cloves garlic, smashed

Turkey Gravy
1 pound turkey legs and/or wings
1½ quarts Chicken Stock
   (see page 227)
1 carrot, rough chopped
1 onion, rough chopped
2 stalks celery, rough chopped
2 cloves garlic, skin intact
4 sprigs thyme
1 bay leaf
½ cup butter
½ cup Wondra flour
½ cup white wine
Salt and pepper

Combine the salt and water in a container large enough to hold the turkey breast. Submerge the turkey in the brine and refrigerate for 24 hours. Remove the breast and discard the liquid.

Heat a large pot of water to 165 degrees on the stovetop. Use a thermometer to ensure the temperature remains constant. It must be maintained throughout the cooking process.

While the water is heating up, seal the turkey breast, buttermilk, thyme and garlic in a large vacuum-seal bag. Submerge the bag into the water. The cold bag will drop the temperature of the water slightly, but it will eventually return to 165 degrees.

Cook the breast for 2 hours and 20 minutes, starting from the time the water temperature rises back to 165 degrees. Check the water temperature periodically and adjust the heat as necessary.

Remove the turkey from the water and allow it to rest in the bag for 10 minutes before slicing.

TURKEY GRAVY
Preheat the oven to 400 degrees. Arrange the turkey parts, onion, carrot, celery and garlic in a single layer in a medium-sized roasting pan or oven-safe pot. Roast for 45 minutes or until the turkey parts are caramelized.

Remove the pan from the oven and place on the stovetop. Over a medium flame, add the wine. Use a large spoon to scrape up any browned bits that have stuck to the bottom of the pan. Add the Chicken Stock and herbs and bring to a boil. Lower the heat and simmer for 1½ hours.

Pass the sauce through a chinois into a clean pot and bring it to a boil. Meanwhile, in a medium-size bowl, knead the butter and flour together with your hands. When the sauce comes to a boil, whisk in the butter-flour mixture. Reduce the flame to simmer and cook for an additional 20 minutes or until the raw flour taste has cooked out. Adjust the seasoning with salt and pepper.

NOTES
SPECIAL EQUIPMENT: Vacuum-seal machine with large bags, thermometer, chinois or fine-mesh strainer.

 WINE PAIRING: The bright, vibrant flavors that a young Pinot Noir delivers are perfect for the rich nature of the Thanksgiving turkey with all the trimmings. Try a basic Bourgogne Rouge.

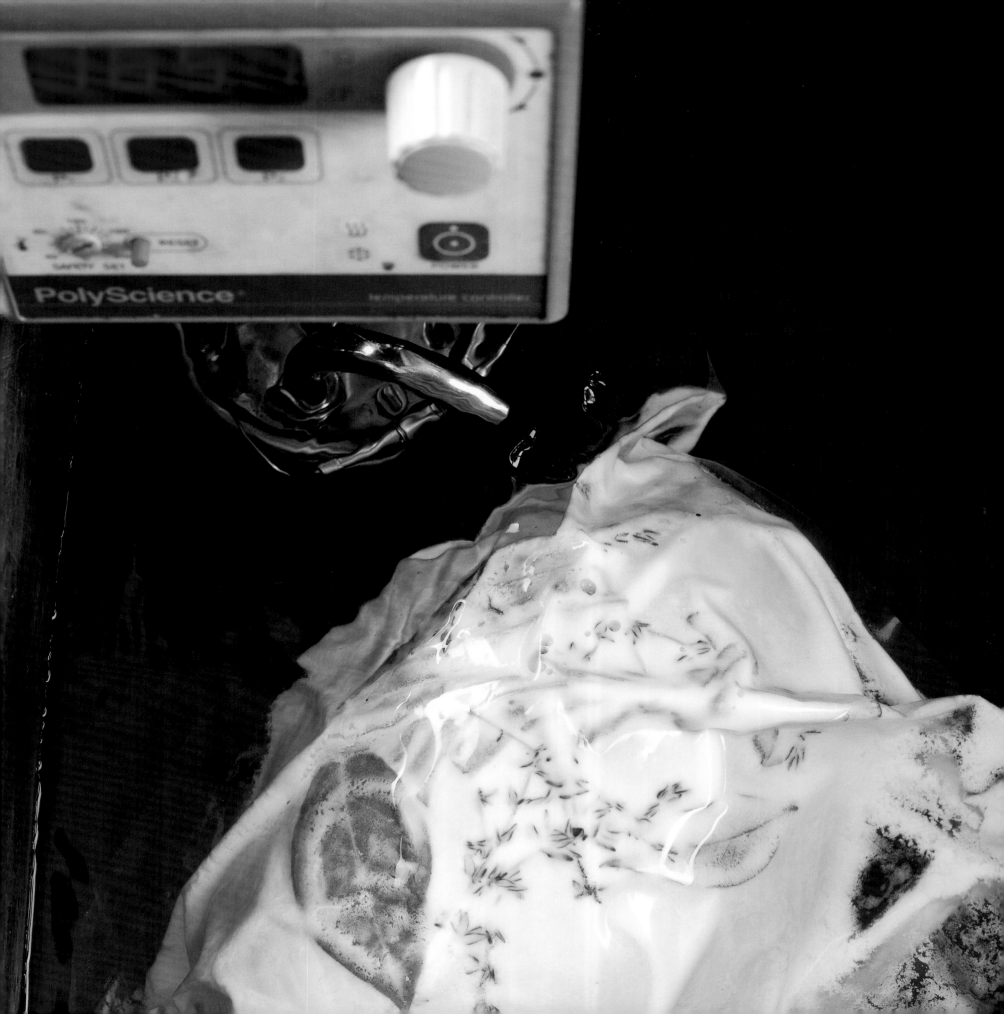

Rib Roast with Potato Gratin and Glazed Carrots Serves Four to Six

Note: When purchasing a rib roast have the butcher tie it for you.

Preheat the oven to 450 degrees. Rub the grapeseed oil into the meat with your hands, then liberally season it with salt and pepper.

Line the bottom of a roasting pan with the chopped vegetables, garlic and thyme. Sit the meat atop the vegetables and roast for 30 minutes. Remove the meat from the oven and lower the oven temperature to 325 degrees.

Deglaze the pan with the red wine, using a wooden spoon to scrape up any of the browned bits stuck to the bottom. Return the pan to the oven and continue roasting until desired temperature is reached. For medium-rare, cook until the internal temperature reaches 120 degrees (for medium, 125 degrees). Start to finish, this will take 45 minutes.

Remove the pan from the oven and allow the meat to rest on a cutting board for at least 10 minutes. The internal temperature will rise as the meat rests.

Remove and discard the string and bone from the roast. Using a sharp carving knife, slice the meat to the desired thickness.

POTATO GRATIN

Preheat the oven to 400 degrees. Combine the cream, garlic and pepper in a large saucepot and bring to a boil. Quickly remove the pot from the heat before the cream boils over.

Ladle enough of the cream mixture into a 9-by-13-inch baking dish to coat the bottom. Using the mandoline, thinly slice the potatoes and layer them in the baking dish. Each layer should use approximately 1½ potatoes. Lightly season the layer with salt. Ladle some cream over the potatoes, just enough to moisten. Repeat this process two more times or until all the potatoes have been used. Pour the remaining cream over the top. Press the top layer down with your hands to help set the potatoes in place.

Cover the baking dish with aluminum foil and bake for 1 hour. Remove the foil and bake for an additional 30 minutes. To check for doneness, pierce the center of the gratin with a paring knife. If the knife passes through with no resistance, the gratin is done.

For best results, make the gratin the day before and refrigerate until ready to use. This will allow the cream and potatoes to completely set, making it easier to handle. If serving the gratin the day it is made, rest it on the countertop for at least 45 minutes. Warm it up in a 400-degree oven for 15 minutes just before serving.

ASSEMBLY

Slice the carrots on a bias into ½-inch pieces and place them in a large pot of cold, salted water. Bring to a boil. Cook the carrots until tender, approximately 5 minutes after the water begins to boil. If not serving immediately, shock the carrots in an ice bath to stop the cooking process and reserve.

Combine the carrots and 1½ cups of water in a medium-sized saucepan and heat over a medium flame. When the water begins to boil, add the butter. Swirl the pan to emulsify the butter into the water. Continue to cook until the liquid has reduced by nearly half. Stir in the parsley and adjust the seasoning with salt

Serve the rib roast, carrots and gratin family style.

NOTES
SPECIAL EQUIPMENT: Mandoline, probe thermometer.

 WINE PAIRING: Pair a Napa Valley Cabernet Sauvignon with this steak-and-potato dish. The sweet fruit and tannic structure of Napa Cabernet Sauvignon brings out the richness of the red meat.

INGREDIENTS

1 bone-in, center-cut beef strip loin (approximately 2–3 pounds)
¼ cup grapeseed oil
½ head garlic, halved and skin intact
1 carrot, rough chopped
½ celery root, rough chopped
1 yellow onion, rough chopped
½ cup red wine
10–12 sprigs thyme, halved
Coarse salt and black pepper

Potato Gratin
6 Yukon Gold potatoes, skin intact, washed
2 cloves garlic, smashed
¼ teaspoon black pepper
1½ tablespoons salt
2 cups heavy cream

Glazed Carrots
12 carrots, peeled
3 tablespoons butter
1½ cups water
2 tablespoons parsley, finely chopped
Salt

Braised Osso Bucco with Roasted Vegetables in Lemon-Parsley Butter Serves Four

INGREDIENTS

4 veal shanks (approximately 1
  pound each)
1 carrot, rough chopped
1 onion, rough chopped
1 stalk celery, rough chopped
½ head garlic, skin intact and
  halved horizontally
2 ripe plum tomatoes
½ cup sherry vinegar
¼ cup tomato paste
1 quart Chicken Stock
  (see page 227)
2 sprigs thyme
1 bay leaf
Wondra flour
Grapeseed oil
Salt and black pepper

Lemon-Parsley Butter

2 tablespoons butter,
  room temperature
1 teaspoon parsley, chopped
½ teaspoon lemon juice

Roasted Carrots
and Fingerling Potatoes

3 cups fingerling potatoes, cut
  into 2-inch medallions
2 cups carrots, cut similarly
  to the potatoes
¼ cup olive oil
2 tablespoons
  Lemon-Parsley Butter
Salt and pepper

Garnish

2 lemons, supremes
2 tablespoons parsley, chopped
Extra-virgin olive oil

Preheat the oven to 350 degrees. Tie each shank with butcher's twine to maintain its shape and keep the bone intact. Pat the shanks dry with a paper towel and liberally season the meat with salt and pepper. Dredge the shanks with Wondra flour and shake of any excess.

Heat a large Dutch oven or oven-safe pot with a lid over medium-high heat. Coat the bottom with grapeseed oil. When the oil is hot, sear the shanks for 5 minutes on each side until nicely browned. Transfer the shanks to a layer of paper towels to remove any excess oil.

Pour off all but 2 tablespoons of oil from the Dutch oven. Add the onions, carrots, celery and garlic, stirring periodically. Sauté until the vegetables start to brown, about 8 minutes. Add the tomatoes and the tomato paste, and cook until the tomatoes break down and the paste begins to brown, approximately 8–10 minutes. Deglaze with the sherry vinegar, using a wooden spoon to loosen all the browned bits stuck to the bottom of the pot.

Add the Chicken Stock and bring to a boil. Add the shanks, thyme and bay leaf. Cover and transfer the pot to the oven. Braise for approximately 2¼ hours. To check for doneness, pierce the widest part of the meat with a paring knife. If the knife pierces through with little to no resistance, the shanks are done.

Remove the pot from the oven. Allow the shanks to rest uncovered at room temperature for at least 1 hour.

Note: The veal shanks can be made a day ahead and refrigerated in the braising liquid overnight.

Remove the shanks from the liquid and set aside. Bring the liquid to a boil. Lower the heat and simmer until the liquid has reduced to a sauce consistency. It should be able to coat the back of a spoon. Pass the sauce through a chinois. Adjust the seasoning with salt and pepper.

LEMON-PARSLEY BUTTER

Combine the ingredients and mix well. Refrigerate until needed.

ROASTED CARROTS AND FINGERLING POTATOES

Preheat the oven to 350 degrees. Toss the potatoes and carrots in the olive oil and season with salt and pepper. Spread out in a single layer on a sheet tray and roast for 30 minutes. When ready to serve, toss the vegetables with the Lemon-Parsley Butter.

ASSEMBLY

Combine the shanks and the sauce in a large pot and gently simmer until the meat is warmed through.

Toss the lemon supremes with the parsley and a few drizzles of extra-virgin olive oil. Serve the shanks family style over the vegetables. Spoon a small amount of the lemon salad on top of each shank.

NOTES

SPECIAL EQUIPMENT: Butcher's twine, Dutch oven (optional), chinois or fine-mesh strainer.

 WINE PAIRING: Osso Bucco needs a wine bold enough to stand up to its full flavors. Wines made in the southern part of Tuscany from the Sangiovese grape, such as a Brunello di Montalcino, are big, earthy, and have substantial tannic acid to cut through the richness of the dish.

The acidity of the parsley butter and lemon supremes balance
the Osso Bucco's richness. Serve the shanks with a small
spoon so your guests can scoop out the marrow.

HORS D'OEUVRES AND SIDE DISHES

Onion Fettuccine   Serves Eight to Ten

INGREDIENTS

2 onions
1 cup heavy cream
2 tablespoons chives, finely
  chopped
Salt and black pepper

Cut each onion in half through the root end, then cut each piece into ½-inch slices to make several half rings. Combine the onion slices with the heavy cream in a medium saucepan and simmer until tender, 8–10 minutes. Season with salt and pepper.

Garnish each serving with a sprinkle of chives.

Parsley Pommes Frites Serves Eight

Ironically, the overwhelming popularity of this item is the reason you will never see it on the menu again. When we did offer it, it wasn't uncommon for a guest to order a triple order of these delicious fries. Several moans and some head shaking from the kitchen crew usually followed. No matter how many orders were prepped ahead of time, it never seemed to be enough. Ask my cooks for an order of Pommes Frites now and they'll tell you where you can stick them!

In 2004, steakhouses helmed by such celebrated chefs as Charlie Palmer and my former employer Jean-Georges Vongerichten were popping up all over New York City. Following the trend, my customers were asking for a steakhouse-style dish. I was hesitant at first. I couldn't visualize this style of entrée on my menu, even at the bar. One of my cooks presented the idea of creating a stylish way to serve the classic steakhouse side Pommes Frites. So we paired it with a steak entrée and put it on the bar menu.

The dish was good, however it was the Pommes Frites that stole the show. People started ordering sides of them at the bar. The conflict was that making the Pommes Frites was extremely time consuming. At the rate they were selling, I was going to have to hire another cook just to prep them out! And I couldn't charge enough money to justify the labor cost. For as much as it makes sense on paper, you can't very well charge someone $15 for a side of fries. Plus, it pained me to no end that I had a bar full of people eating what was in essence French fries.

So I started denying people their requests for side orders. If you wanted the Pommes Frites, you had to order the entire entrée. Eventually, I took the Pommes Frites off the menu. A large number of Pommes-Frites enthusiasts were heartbroken to see them go (you know who you are), so to appease their loss, here's the damn recipe. Make a triple order for yourself.

PARSLEY BUTTER

Combine all ingredients in a medium bowl and mix thoroughly until fully incorporated. Refrigerate until needed.

Note: Parsley Butter can be made ahead and refrigerated for up to a week.

POMMES FRITES

Preheat the deep fryer to 300 degrees or heat the canola oil in a large heavy-bottomed saucepot to that temperature.

Cut each potato lengthwise into thirds. Then trim each piece into rectangles, approximately 2 inches long and ½ inch thick. Hold the pieces in cold water until all the potatoes have been cut to size to prevent them from oxidizing.

Dry the potatoes as much as possible with paper towels. Working in batches, blanch them in the oil for 3 minutes. They should not brown at this stage. Remove them from the fryer and allow them to drain on a few layers of paper towels.

Raise the oil temperature to 325 degrees. Fry the blanched potatoes for 3 minutes or until golden brown. Remove them from the oil and allow them to drain on paper towels. Transfer the fried potatoes to a large bowl. Season with salt and pepper and toss with approximately 3 tablespoons of Parsley Butter. Stack the Pommes Frites on a plate and serve.

NOTES
SPECIAL EQUIPMENT: Home deep fryer or deep-fry thermometer.

INGREDIENTS

Parsley Butter
1 tablespoon shallots, finely chopped
1 clove garlic, finely chopped
½ cup parsley, finely chopped
8 ounces butter, softened
Salt

Pommes Frites
8 large russet potatoes
Canola oil, as needed for deep frying
Salt and black pepper

Lobster Salad with
Grilled Scallions on Crispy Wontons Serves Eight to Ten

INGREDIENTS

Sherry Mayonnaise
1 egg yolk
2 cups canola oil, chilled
⅓ cup sherry vinegar
Salt and white pepper

Fried Wontons
1 package wonton wrappers
Canola oil, for deep frying
Salt

Lobster Salad
4 scallions, green part only
2 cups cooked lobster meat,
    chopped
Sherry Mayonnaise
Grapeseed oil
2 scallions, green part only, thinly
    sliced on the bias
2 oranges, supremed
Salt and black pepper

SHERRY MAYONNAISE
Place the egg yolk and a tablespoon of the vinegar in a food processor. With the blade running on high, slowly drizzle in the oil. When all of the oil has been incorporated, add the rest of the vinegar. Adjust the seasoning with salt and pepper. Refrigerate until needed.

Note: Sherry Mayonnaise can be made ahead and refrigerated for up to a week.

FRIED WONTONS
Preheat a deep fryer to 300 degrees or heat canola oil in a large saucepot to 300 degrees. Punch out rounds from the wontons with the ring mold. Working in batches, fry the wonton rounds until crispy and golden brown. Transfer the fried wonton rounds to a tray lined with paper towels to remove any excess oil. Season the wontons with salt immediately after they come out of the oil.

LOBSTER SALAD
Preheat a grill or stovetop grill pan to medium heat. Coat 4 scallions with grapeseed oil and salt. Grill the scallions just until they are slightly charred. Remove from the grill and let cool. Slice the scallions into thin pieces.

In a medium bowl, combine the lobster and the grilled scallions. Fold in enough Sherry Mayonnaise to bind the salad. Season with salt and pepper.

Top each wonton with a bit of the salad. Garnish each hors d'oeuvre with an orange supreme.

NOTES
SPECIAL EQUIPMENT: 2-inch ring mold, deep-fry thermometer or home deep fryer.

Potato Pancakes
with Bacon and Quince Puree Serves Eight to Ten

Peel the potatoes and grate them directly into a bowl of cold water. Allow the grated potato to rest in the water for 10 minutes to release its starch.

Meanwhile, grate the onion and reserve.

Gently lift the grated potato from the bowl and squeeze out as much water as possible. Let the starchy water settle for 5 minutes. Mix the egg yolks and grated onion with the potatoes and season with salt and pepper.

A layer of potato starch should have settled at the bottom of the bowl. Carefully pour out the water, leaving the starch behind. Fold the starch into the potato-onion mixture.

Lay a piece of plastic wrap approximately 15 inches long horizontally across your work surface. Line the potato mixture in a long strip across the middle of the plastic wrap. Fold the bottom half of the plastic over to the top half. Roll the potato mixture up firmly in the plastic and twist the ends to tighten it. The result should be a tightly wrapped cylinder 2 inches in diameter. Transfer the cylinder to the freezer until completely solid.

Remove the potato cylinder from the freezer and defrost at room temperature for 10 minutes or until it can be easily sliced with a knife while retaining its shape. Remove the plastic wrap and slice into ¼-inch rounds. Lay the rounds flat on a sheet tray and refreeze them.

Note: The potato pancakes can be made ahead, frozen completely and stored in a plastic container for up to 6 months.

QUINCE PUREE
Combine the quince and poaching liquid in a pot and warm through on medium-low heat. Transfer to a blender and puree on high until smooth.

Note: Quince Puree can be made ahead and refrigerated for up to 3 days.

ASSEMBLY
Cook the bacon slices in a sauté pan until crispy. Drain on paper towels. Chop the bacon into a fine crumble. Reserve.

Set the fryer to 325 degrees or heat the oil in a heavy-bottomed pot to that temperature. Working in batches, fry the frozen potato pancakes for 2–3 minutes or until golden brown. Season immediately with salt and allow to drain on paper towels.

Spoon a dollop of Quince Puree on each pancake and top with chopped bacon and chives.

NOTES
SPECIAL EQUIPMENT: Box grater, home deep fryer or deep-fry thermometer.

INGREDIENTS

2 large russet potatoes
2 egg yolks, lightly beaten
¼ white onion
Salt and pepper

Quince Puree
2 Poached Quince (see page 138)
½ cup quince poaching liquid

Assembly
4–5 slices bacon
¼ cup chives, finely chopped
Canola oil, as needed for
  deep frying
Salt

Shrimp Tempura with Spicy Soy Sauce Serves Eight to Ten

INGREDIENTS

Spicy Soy Sauce

1 cup soy sauce
2 tablespoons mirin
1 tablespoon rice wine vinegar
2 Thai chilies
2 tablespoons sugar
1 tablespoon cornstarch
¼ cup water

Tempura Batter

1 cup cake flour
¼ cup cornstarch
½ tablespoon salt
2 teaspoons baking powder
1¼ cups club soda, cold

Shrimp

16 shrimp (16/20 size), peeled,
  deveined and cut into thirds
Canola oil, as needed for
  deep frying
Salt

SPICY SOY SAUCE

Combine the soy sauce, mirin, rice wine vinegar, Thai chilies and sugar in a medium-sized pot. Cook over medium heat until the sugar is dissolved, stirring occasionally.

Meanwhile, combine the cornstarch and water to make a slurry. Bring the soy sauce mixture to a boil and whisk in the slurry to thicken it to a sauce consistency. Be sure to simmer the sauce for at least 2 minutes to ensure the raw starch is cooked out.

Pass the sauce through a fine-mesh strainer and reserve.

Note: Spicy Soy Sauce can be made ahead and refrigerated for up to a week. Bring it to room temperature before serving.

TEMPURA BATTER

Mix together the dry ingredients and whisk in the club soda until the consistency of loose pancake batter is reached.

ASSEMBLY

Set the deep fryer to 325 degrees or heat approximately 2 quarts of canola oil in a heavy-bottomed pot to that temperature. Pierce each piece of shrimp with a skewer. Holding the skewer, dip the shrimp into the tempura batter, shake off any excess, and immediately transfer to the hot oil. Fry until the tempura puffs up, about 2 minutes. Remove the shrimp from the fryer and drain on paper towels. Season with salt.

Arrange the shrimp skewers on a tray. The Spicy Soy Sauce can either be placed in a vessel or spooned over the shrimp.

NOTES

SPECIAL EQUIPMENT: Wooden skewers, home deep fryer or deep-fry thermometer.

Curry Marinated Lamb with Curry Yogurt Serves Eight to Ten

Toast the curry in a dry sauté pan over low heat for about 2 minutes or until fragrant. Reserve half the curry for the yogurt sauce. Combine the other half with the olive oil and salt.

Dry the lamb loin with a kitchen towel to remove any excess moisture. Slice the loin lengthwise into 4 long strips. Slice the strips into bite-size cubes. Mix the lamb with the curry oil and allow it to marinate in the refrigerator for at least 2 hours.

CURRY YOGURT SAUCE
Combine the yogurt and the toasted curry. Adjust the seasoning with salt and pepper.

Note: Curry Yogurt Sauce can be made ahead and refrigerated for up to 3 days.

ASSEMBLY
Pierce each lamb cube with a wooden skewer. Heat a large sauté pan over medium-high heat and coat the bottom with grapeseed oil. Place the lamb in the pan with the skewers sitting outside the lip of the pan. Sear the lamb on each side for 1–2 minutes for medium. A griddle pan would also work well.

Line the skewers decoratively on a large serving platter. The Curry Yogurt Sauce can be either placed in a vessel for dipping or spooned onto the plate.

NOTES
SPECIAL EQUIPMENT: Wooden skewers.

INGREDIENTS

1 lamb loin, trimmed (approximately 2½–3 pounds)
3 tablespoons Madras curry powder
1 cup olive oil
½ tablespoon salt
Grapeseed oil

Curry Yogurt Sauce
1½ cups plain yogurt
1½ tablespoons Madras curry powder, toasted
Salt and pepper

Asparagus Crostini
with Parmesan and Truffle Vinaigrette Serves Eight to Ten

INGREDIENTS

1 baguette

1 bunch asparagus, peeled and
  trimmed

1 cup Parmesan, grated

1 tablespoon champagne vinegar

¼ cup plus 1 tablespoon extra-
  virgin olive oil, divided

½ tablespoon truffle oil

2 tablespoons black truffles,
  chopped (optional)

Salt and pepper

Preheat the oven to 325 degrees. Using a sharp serrated knife, thinly slice the baguette on the bias. Toss the bread slices with ¼ cup olive oil, salt and pepper in a large bowl. Arrange the slices on a sheet pan lined with parchment paper and bake until they are light golden and crispy, about 10 minutes. Allow the crostini to cool on paper towels at room temperature.

Bring a large pot of salted water to a boil. Blanch the asparagus 2–3 minutes or until tender then immediately shock it in an ice bath. When completely cooled, allow the asparagus to dry on paper towels. Slice the asparagus with a sharp knife on a slight bias.

Whisk together the vinegar, remaining olive oil, truffle oil and chopped truffles (if available) in a small bowl. Reserve the vinaigrette until needed.

ASSEMBLY

Raise the oven to 350 degrees. Lay the toasted bread slices on a sheet pan lined with parchment paper. Toss the sliced asparagus with the vinaigrette and adjust the seasoning with salt, if necessary. Spoon approximately 1 teaspoon of asparagus salad on top of each crostini. Sprinkle with grated Parmesan. Bake for 5 minutes, just to warm through. Arrange the crostini on a platter and serve family style.

Chicken Satay Skewers with Peanut Dressing Serves Eight to Ten

Whisk together the soy sauce, brown sugar and chili sauce until the sugar is completely dissolved. Slice the chicken into bite-size cubes and marinate them in the soy mixture for at least 2 hours.

PEANUT DRESSING

Place a medium-sized saucepot over medium heat. When the pan is hot, add the ketchup and cook for approximately 20 seconds. Deglaze the pot with the vinegar and scrape up any ketchup stuck to the pot with a wooden spoon. Add the peanut butter and chili sauce and mix well. Adjust the consistency with water. The sauce should be suitable for dipping. Season with salt. Refrigerate until needed.

Note: Peanut Dressing can be made ahead and stored in the refrigerator for up to 3 days.

ASSEMBLY

Pierce each chicken cube with a wooden skewer. Heat a large sauté pan over medium-high heat. When the pan is hot, coat the bottom with grapeseed oil. Place the chicken into the pan with the skewers pointing outward. Cook the chicken on each side for 2–3 minutes or until fully cooked.

Serve the satays on a large platter. The sauce can either be placed in a vessel for dipping or spooned onto the platter.

NOTES
SPECIAL EQUIPMENT: Wooden skewers.

INGREDIENTS

2 boneless, skinless chicken
   breasts
1 cup soy sauce
1 tablespoon brown sugar
¼ cup sweet chili sauce (for
   Asian spring rolls)
Grapeseed oil

Peanut Dressing

1 cup peanut butter
¼ cup sweet chili sauce (for
   Asian spring rolls)
2 tablespoons ketchup
¼ cup rice wine vinegar
½ cup water
Salt

COCKTAILS

Pineapple Mojito Serves One

INGREDIENTS

2 tablespoons fresh chopped
   pineapple
3 sprigs mint
2 tablespoons Brown Sugar
   Simple Syrup
2 ounces spiced rum
Club soda

Brown Sugar Simple Syrup
1 cup water
1 cup dark brown sugar

BROWN SUGAR SIMPLE SYRUP

Combine the sugar and the water in a medium saucepot. Heat on medium flame until the sugar is completely dissolved. Let the syrup cool to room temperature then store it in the refrigerator.

ASSEMBLY

Thoroughly muddle the mint and pineapple in a shaker. Add the rum and Brown Sugar Simple Syrup. Shake and pour into a tall glass filled with ice. Top off with club soda. Garnish with a slice of fresh pineapple.

Drunken Cranberry Mojito Serves One

MACERATED CRANBERRIES

Place cranberries in a small bowl and cover with rum. Refrigerate for at least 2 days. This will yield enough macerated cranberries for 4 drinks.

ASSEMBLY

In a shaker, thoroughly muddle the mint, cranberries and lime juice. Fill the shaker with ice, rum, Simple Syrup and cranberry juice. Shake and transfer to a tall glass. Top off with additional ice and club soda.

INGREDIENTS

4 sprigs mint
1 tablespoon Macerated
  Cranberries
Juice of ¼ lime
1 tablespoon Simple Syrup
  (see page 230)
1½ ounces spiced rum (such as
  Mount Gay or Montecristo)
Splash of cranberry juice
Club soda

Macerated Cranberries

¼ cup dried cranberries
½ cup spiced rum (such as
  Mount Gay or Montecristo)

Strawberry Basil Mojito Serves One

STRAWBERRY SIMPLE SYRUP

Place the sugar, water and strawberries into a saucepot. Bring to a boil then reduce to a simmer. Cook for 10 minutes and strain. Discard the strawberries. Refrigerate the syrup until needed.

ASSEMBLY

In a shaker, thoroughly muddle the basil, strawberries, Strawberry Simple Syrup and lime juice. Add rum and fill with ice. Shake and transfer to a tall glass. Top off with additional ice and club soda.

INGREDIENTS

4 sprigs basil
strawberries
Juice of ¼ lime
1 tablespoon Strawberry
  Simple Syrup
1½ ounces Bacardi light rum
Club soda

Strawberry Simple Syrup

1 cup chopped strawberries
1 cup sugar
1½ cups water

Pear Thyme Crush Serves One

PEAR PUREE
Combine the pears and Simple Syrup in a heavy-bottomed saucepan and bring to a boil. Remove from heat and let the pears steep in the syrup until soft.

Remove the pears from the syrup and puree in a blender until smooth. Refrigerate until needed.

Fill a shaker halfway with crushed ice and add the tequila, lime juice, Pear Puree and a few thyme leaves. Depending on the sweetness of the pears, you may need to add a splash of Simple Syrup. Shake and pour into a rocks glass.

INGREDIENTS

2 ounces tequila
Juice from ¼ lime
Thyme leaves
2 ounces Pear Puree

Pear Puree
2 ripe pears, peeled, seeded
  and quartered
1 cup Simple Syrup
  (see page 230)

Mango Crush Serves One

MANGO PUREE
Combine the mango and Simple Syrup in a heavy-bottomed saucepan and bring to a boil. Remove from heat and let the mangos steep in the syrup until soft.

Remove the mangos from the syrup and puree in a blender until smooth. Refrigerate until needed.

ASSEMBLY
Fill a shaker halfway with crushed ice and add the tequila, lime juice and Mango Puree. Depending on the sweetness of the mangos, you may need to add an extra splash of Simple Syrup. Shake and pour into a rocks glass.

INGREDIENTS

2 ounces tequila
Juice from ¼ lime
2 ounces Mango Puree

Mango Puree
1 ripe mango, peeled and cut into
  small pieces
1 cup Simple Syrup
  (see page 230)

Peach Crush Serves One

PEACH PUREE
Combine the peach and Simple Syrup in a heavy-bottomed saucepan and bring it to a boil. Turn off the heat and let the peaches steep in the syrup until soft.

Remove the peaches from the syrup and puree them in a blender until smooth. Refrigerate until needed.

ASSEMBLY
Fill a shaker halfway with crushed ice. Add the tequila, lime juice and Peach Puree. Depending on the sweetness of the peaches, you may need to add a splash of Simple Syrup. Shake and pour into a rocks glass.

INGREDIENTS

2 ounces tequila
Juice from ¼ lime
2 ounces Peach Puree

Peach Puree
2 ripe peaches, peeled,
  medium dice
1 cup Simple Syrup
  (see page 230)

Autumn Apple Martini <small>Serves One</small>

INGREDIENTS

1 ounce Southern Comfort
1 ounce Licor 43
1 ounce apple schnapps
3 ounces apple cider
1 slice of apple for garnish

Combine all the ingredients in a shaker filled with ice. Shake and strain into a chilled martini glass. Garnish with the apple slice.

Grapefruit Martini <small>Serves One</small>

INGREDIENTS

2 ounces vodka
4 ounces fresh grapefruit juice
Simple Syrup (see page 230),
  optional

If the grapefruit juice is a little bitter, a little Simple Syrup can be added. Combine the vodka and grapefruit juice in a shaker and fill with ice. Shake and strain into a chilled martini glass.

Cantaloupe Martini <small>Serves One</small>

INGREDIENTS

2 ounces vodka
4 ounces fresh cantaloupe juice
Simple Syrup (see page 230),
  optional

Be sure the cantaloupe is ripe before juicing. If it's not sweet enough, add a little Simple Syrup. Fill a shaker with ice, vodka and cantaloupe juice. Shake well and strain into a chilled martini glass.

NOTES
SPECIAL EQUIPMENT: Electric fruit/vegetable juicer.

Autumn Apple Martini

Berry Soup with Yogurt Sorbet Serves Eight

INGREDIENTS

Yogurt Sorbet

4 cups plain yogurt
¾ cup sugar
¾ cup corn syrup
1 vanilla bean or 1 teaspoon
   vanilla extract

Berry Soup

2 pints blueberries
2 pints raspberries
1 pint blackberries
2 cups water
1 cup sugar
½ cup fresh basil leaves
1 vanilla bean, scraped
Lemon juice

YOGURT SORBET

Combine all ingredients in a heavy-bottomed, medium-sized saucepot. Gently warm through on medium-low heat until the sugar has dissolved, stirring occasionally. Strain the mixture through a fine-mesh strainer then cool it in the refrigerator. Spin the sorbet in an ice cream machine using the manufacturer's instructions. Store in the freezer until needed.

BERRY SOUP

Combine all the ingredients except for the lemon juice in a heavy-bottomed saucepot. Bring to a boil then remove from the heat. Allow all the flavors to infuse for 30 minutes.

Thoroughly puree the berry mixture in a blender. Strain the soup through a fine-mesh strainer. The tartness of the fruit will determine how much lemon juice is needed, if any at all. Taste the soup and stir in lemon juice to balance the sweetness. Refrigerate until completely cooled.

ASSEMBLY

Ladle the desired amount of soup into a chilled bowl. Float a scoop of Yogurt Sorbet in the center. Garnish with fresh berries and a sprig of mint. Serve with your favorite wafer cookie, if desired.

NOTES

SPECIAL EQUIPMENT: Ice cream machine, fine-mesh strainer.

Chocolate Soufflé Serves Six

Preheat the oven to 450 degrees. Bring a large pot of water to a boil. Place a stainless steel bowl on top of the pot to create a double boiler. (The bowl should not touch the water.) Melt the chocolate pieces, stirring occasionally.

With the stand mixer on medium speed, whip the egg whites and sugar into stiff peaks. Remove the bowl of melted chocolate from the double boiler and stir in the egg yolks. Gently fold in the egg whites, being careful not to over mix.

Coat the interior of the soufflé molds with butter. Dust with granulated sugar and shake off any excess. Fill the molds completely with batter and bake in the oven for 5 minutes. Serve immediately with vanilla ice cream (optional).

NOTES

SPECIAL EQUIPMENT: Electric stand mixer with whip attachment, 6 3-inch soufflé molds.

INGREDIENTS

6 eggs yolks
200 grams Valrhona Caraibe
    chocolate
6 egg whites
50 grams granulated sugar, plus
    additional sugar for
    dusting molds
Butter

Coconut Tapioca Soup with Passion Fruit Sauce Serves Six

INGREDIENTS

Coconut Tapioca Soup
5 cups whole milk
½ cup sugar
½ cup tapioca
1 13½-ounce can coconut milk

Passion Fruit Sauce
4 cups passion fruit puree
1 cup sugar

Crystallized Mint
1 cup mint, packed
1 egg white
¼ cup granulated sugar

COCONUT TAPIOCA SOUP

Combine the milk and sugar in a large heavy-bottomed pot and simmer over medium heat until sugar is dissolved, stirring continuously. Reduce the flame to its lowest setting and add the tapioca. Continue to gently simmer for approximately 40 minutes, stirring occasionally.

Add the coconut milk and simmer for an additional 2 minutes. Transfer the soup to another container and refrigerate until completely cooled.

PASSION FRUIT SAUCE

In a heavy-bottomed saucepot, bring the puree and sugar to a boil. Reduce the heat and simmer for approximately 20 minutes, stirring occasionally. The sauce should be reduced by nearly half.

CRYSTALLIZED MINT

Lightly brush both sides of the mint leaves with egg white. Toss the leaves with the sugar and lay them out on a sheet tray lined with a rack. Place the tray in a cool, dry place for 1–3 days, depending on the relative humidity. When the mint is fully dehydrated, grind it into a fine powder using a spice grinder.

ASSEMBLY

Spoon approximately ¼ cup of the Passion Fruit Syrup into a shallow bowl. Pour the Coconut Tapioca Soup over the syrup. Garnish with a sprinkle of Crystallized Mint.

NOTES

SPECIAL EQUIPMENT: Electric spice grinder, pastry brush.

This delicious soup works equally well as a dessert course unto itself or, in a smaller portion, as a teaser before the main event. In fact, it is one of the most popular dessert amuse-bouches at the restaurant. Passion fruit puree can be found at gourmet shops and high-end supermarkets.

Banana Bread Yields Eight Individual Loaves or Two Large Loaves

We used to present a small tray of petit fours to our guests after their meal. Nothing excessive, just a small little something to let you know that we were glad you could join us for the evening. They ranged from little chocolates to mini-marshmallows. I noticed, though, that only half of the guests would eat them. It wasn't because they weren't good—in fact, they were delicious—but after a big meal, people just couldn't eat another bite. Anne, my pastry chef, spent a good portion of her week preparing these small confections and half were going to waste! It was an issue.

So we came up with the idea that every lady, before leaving us for the evening, would receive a mini loaf of bread presented in a bag custom made to resemble a little Gucci purse. The bread could be sliced up for a midnight snack or eaten in the morning for breakfast. This way our guests would be reminded of the previous evening and not a morsel would go to waste. The breads, which come in a variety of seasonal flavors, have since become a signature of Restaurant Nicholas.

INGREDIENTS

2⅓ cups sugar
1¼ cups butter
1 teaspoon salt
5 eggs
10 medium ripe bananas
2¾ cups flour
1½ tablespoons baking soda

Combine the sugar and butter in the bowl of the stand mixer. Mix on the lowest setting until smooth and creamy, about 10 minutes, scraping down the paddle and sides of the bowl with a rubber spatula as necessary.

Add the eggs, one at a time, scraping down the sides of the bowl after each one.

Puree bananas in a food processor until smooth and add them to the mixer. Increase the mixer's speed by one and mix for about 10 minutes. Sift the flour and baking soda and add them to the mixer. Mix until the flour is fully incorporated, then stop. Do not over mix.

Preheat the oven to 350 degrees. Spray the interior of the loaf pans with nonstick cooking spray. Fill the pans ¾ full and place them on a sheet tray. For the individual loaves, bake for 30 minutes, then rotate the tray and bake for an additional 30 minutes. For the larger loaves, bake in 35-minute increments.

The bread can be served warm or at room temperature. When cooled, it can be wrapped and refrigerated for up to 3 days.

NOTES
SPECIAL EQUIPMENT: 8 5½-inch-by-3-inch loaf pans or 2 9-inch-by-5-inch loaf pans, electric stand mixer with paddle attachment, fine-mesh tamis or flour sifter.

These particular recipes translate really well for the home kitchen. The loaves can be baked in advance and stored for a few days.

Pumpkin Bread
Yields Five Individual Loaves or One Large Loaf

Preheat the oven to 350 degrees.

Combine the sugars in the stand mixer's bowl and mix on the lowest setting to eliminate any lumps. Add the oil and mix until smooth, approximately 10 minutes.

Add the eggs, one at a time. After each egg, stop the mixer and scrape down the sides with a rubber spatula. When all the eggs have been incorporated, add the vanilla extract and the pumpkin puree. Mix thoroughly, about 10 minutes.

Sift the dry ingredients and add them to the batter. Mix until they are just incorporated.

Spray the interior of the loaf pan(s) with nonstick cooking spray and fill it ¾ full. Place the pan(s) on a sheet tray. For the individual loaves, bake for 30 minutes, then rotate the tray and bake for an additional 30 minutes. For the larger loaf, bake in 35-minute increments.

The bread can be served warm or at room temperature. When cooled, it can be wrapped and refrigerated for up to 3 days.

NOTES
SPECIAL EQUIPMENT: 5 5½-inch-by-3-inch loaf pans or 1 9-inch-by-5-inch loaf pan, electric stand mixer with paddle attachment, fine-mesh tamis or flour sifter.

INGREDIENTS

1 cup light brown sugar
1 cup granulated sugar
1 cup canola oil
4 eggs
3 cups all-purpose flour
1 teaspoon ground ginger
1½ teaspoons ground cinnamon
½ teaspoon nutmeg
1 teaspoon ground cloves
1 teaspoon salt
½ teaspoon baking powder
1 teaspoon baking soda
1 teaspoon vanilla extract
2 cups canned pumpkin puree

If you don't want to go through the trouble of making the chicory ice cream, a store-bought coffee ice cream can be substituted. Alternatively, you can serve the beignets with coffee for a sweet breakfast or late-night snack.

Beignets with Chicory Ice Cream Serves Eight

When most people go on vacation they bring back souvenirs, like T-shirts and bumper stickers. I return home with recipes. Beignets with Chicory Ice Cream, one of Restaurant Nicholas's most celebrated desserts, stemmed from a trip to New Orleans in March 2005.

The people of New Orleans are some of the nicest, most genuine people around. They aren't shy in telling you where to eat, where to find the best music, and even where not to go. Besides its great cuisine, New Orleans is saturated with rich history and folklore, especially that involving ghosts and voodoo. Like many vacationers, we went on ghost tours and trips to the city's famous above-ground cemeteries. Although a little hokey, some of those ghost stories were a little disturbing.

In between touring haunted houses, Melissa and I ate our way around the city. On our list of places to eat was Café Du Monde, a New Orleans institution since 1862. Open 24 hours a day and patronized by tourists and locals alike, it's famous for its beignets and café au lait blended with chicory.

Late one evening, after a long day of food, ghosts and live music, we decided that coffee and donuts would be the perfect cap to the night. Following a local gentleman's directions, spoken in a heavy Cajun accent, we made our way to Decatur Street. As we walked, a thick fog rolled in off the Mississippi. You could barely see your hand in front of your face. The old-fashioned gas lamps cast an eerie glow on the deserted street as I tried to remember the areas where we were told to steer clear. We didn't want to admit it, but the ghost stories were getting to us.

After what seemed like an eternity, we finally saw a light at the end of the fog: Café Du Monde. We made it!

Café Du Monde is an old, rundown shack of a building. The interior is covered with powdered sugar. At 2:30 am, the place was mobbed with people and I could see why. The powdery treats were out of this world.

Along with an extra 10 pounds, I returned from New Orleans with the idea to recreate Café Du Monde's classic beignets and chicory coffee as an elegant dessert. Our version replaced the hot café au lait with chicory ice cream, and our donuts were smaller and more uniform. Our customers really seemed to like them since they ended up being one of our most popular desserts.

A few months later, Hurricane Katrina forced Café Du Monde to close its doors on a day other than Christmas for the first time in its history. Thankfully, it only suffered minor damage and reopened two months later.

We took the beignets off the menu after Katrina. I felt it was the right thing to do. Many customers were sad to see them go. After much coaxing, they returned and stayed on the menu for nearly two years. Eventually it was time to retire the beignets, but surprisingly we still get requests for them.

In the stand mixer's bowl, dissolve the yeast in the warm water, approximately 5 minutes. Add the rest of the ingredients except for the powdered sugar to the bowl and mix for 10 minutes.

Spray a large bowl with nonstick cooking spray. Place the dough into the bowl and cover with plastic wrap. Allow the dough to rise in a cool, dry place for 6 hours.

Invert the dough onto a floured work surface. Roll the dough out approximately ½ inch thick. Cut the dough into 2-inch-by-2-inch squares and transfer them to a sheet tray dusted heavily with flour. Wrap and refrigerate until needed.

INGREDIENTS

¼ ounce active dry yeast
6 ounces warm water
2 ounces sugar
17 ounces all-purpose flour, sifted
1 egg
½ cup milk
4 tablespoons butter
½ teaspoon salt
3 tablespoons powdered sugar

continues »

Chicory Ice Cream

2 cups half-and-half

½ cup milk

5 egg yolks

½ cup plus 1½ tablespoons
   sugar

1 tablespoon plus ½ teaspoon
   chicory

½ teaspoon plus ¼ teaspoon
   coffee paste

CHICORY ICE CREAM

In a medium-sized bowl, whisk the egg yolks, half the sugar and the coffee paste. Place the half-and-half, milk, chicory and the remainder of the sugar in a heavy-bottomed saucepot. Bring to a boil. Reduce the heat and simmer for 5 minutes, stirring constantly. Remove the pot from the heat.

Temper the egg mixture by slowly ladling about $\frac{1}{2}$ cup of the hot liquid into the eggs while whisking constantly. Pour the remainder of the liquid into the eggs then return the mixture to the pot.

Fill a large bowl with ice and water. Put a smaller bowl on top. Strain the ice cream base through a fine-mesh strainer into the bowl. Stir frequently until the base is completely cooled.

Spin the base through an ice cream machine using the manufacturer's instructions.

ASSEMBLY

Preheat the deep fryer to 325 degrees. Fry the beignets until golden brown. Allow them to drain briefly then toss with powdered sugar. Serve with the Chicory Ice Cream.

NOTES

SPECIAL EQUIPMENT: Electric stand mixer with paddle attachment, ice cream machine, electric deep fryer, fine-mesh strainer, tamis or flour sifter.

Valrhona Chocolate Cake
with Vanilla Ice Cream Yields Twelve 2-Ounce Cakes or Six 4-Ounce Cakes

In New York City circa the late '80s/early '90s, molten chocolate cake was on every dessert menu. Talk to the pastry chefs from that era and you will receive conflicting stories on who the originator was. For me, the credit goes to Eric Hubert, the former pastry chef of Jean Georges. When I was opening Restaurant Nicholas, Eric was the consulting pastry chef. Along with many of his ideas and concepts, the chocolate cake is a staple on our dessert menu.

Of all our menu items, this recipe is the most sought after by our customers. There are countless versions of this dessert, and while we have modified the accompaniments over the years, the basic recipe still stands.

INGREDIENTS

5 eggs
5 egg yolks
125 grams sugar
250 grams butter, cut into
    small cubes
250 grams Valrhona chocolate,
    rough chopped
50 grams flour, sifted
Butter and flour, as needed
    for molds

Vanilla Ice Cream
4 cups half-and-half
1 cup milk
3 vanilla beans, split
10 egg yolks
25 grams sugar

Liberally coat each mold with softened butter and dust with flour. Shake off any excess. Refrigerate the molds to set the butter.

Set up a double boiler by placing a metal or glass bowl over a large pot of boiling water. The bowl should not touch the water. Melt the chocolate and butter in the bowl, stirring occasionally.

While the chocolate is melting, combine the eggs and sugar in the stand mixer's bowl and whip them at medium speed for approximately 10 minutes. Stop the mixer and scrape down the sides of the bowl with a spatula as necessary.

Stop the mixer and add half of the melted chocolate to the bowl. Mix for another 2 minutes on medium speed. Scrape down the sides and add the remaining chocolate. Mix for an additional 2 minutes. Stop the mixer and add the flour. Mix on low speed for 30 seconds.

Ladle the chocolate mixture into the buttered molds. Refrigerate the molds overnight to allow the chocolate to set.

Preheat the oven to 425 degrees. Place the cakes on a sheet pan and bake for 6 minutes. Invert the chocolate cake onto a plate and remove the mold. Dust with powdered sugar and serve with vanilla ice cream.

VANILLA ICE CREAM
Using the back of a paring knife, scrape out the seeds of each vanilla bean. Combine the milk, half-and-half, vanilla beans and the vanilla seeds in a heavy-bottomed saucepot. Bring to a gentle simmer.

Whisk the sugar and egg yolks together in a large bowl. While continuing to mix, ladle some of the hot milk mixture over the yolks to temper them. When the milk is fully incorporated into the yolks, add them to the milk on the stovetop. Cook over low heat, stirring frequently.

The ice cream base is done when it is thick enough to coat the back of a spoon. Strain the mixture through a fine-mesh strainer and refrigerate. When completely chilled, spin through an ice cream machine using the manufacturer's instructions.

NOTES
SPECIAL EQUIPMENT: Electric stand mixer with whisk attachment, 12 2-ounce cake molds or 6 4-ounce cake molds, ice cream machine, tamis or flour sifter.

The ingredients are measured in grams to keep them as exact as possible. We have provided a recipe for our vanilla ice cream, though a store-bought version can be substituted.

Vanilla Crème Brûlée Serves Six

Combine all ingredients in a large bowl and whisk together vigorously. Strain through a fine-mesh strainer to remove the whole vanilla beans.

Preheat the oven to 375 degrees. Fill each ramekin with the egg-and-cream mixture and place into a large baking dish. Fill the dish with enough warm water so that the ramekins are half submerged. Lightly torch the tops of the ramekins to remove any air bubbles. Cover the baking dish with foil. Bake for approximately 20 minutes. Carefully rotate the pan and bake for an additional 20 minutes.

Remove the baking pan from the oven. Discard the foil and let the custard-filled ramekins rest at room temperature for 30 minutes to set. Remove the ramekins from the water and refrigerate to cool completely.

The custards can be made ahead, wrapped in plastic and refrigerated for up to 3 days.

ASSEMBLY
Cover the top layer of the custard with granulated sugar and wipe the rim of any excess. Torch the top layer until the sugar caramelizes.

ESPRESSO CRÈME BRÛLÉE
Follow the same procedure as for Vanilla Crème Brûlée, but substitute 1 ounce of cold double decaf espresso for the vanilla beans.

NUTMEG CRÈME BRÛLÉE
Follow the same procedure as for Vanilla Crème Brûlée, but substitute ½ teaspoon of grated nutmeg for the vanilla beans.

NOTES
SPECIAL EQUIPMENT: 6 4-ounce oven-safe shallow ramekins, propane blow torch, fine-mesh strainer.

INGREDIENTS

5 egg yolks
2 cups heavy cream
⅓ cup plus 1 tablespoon sugar
1½ vanilla beans, split
   and scraped
Sugar

Brown Butter Yields 1 Pound

INGREDIENTS

1 pound butter

Melt the butter in a large, heavy-bottomed pot over medium heat. Continue cooking the butter until it gets dark brown but not burnt. Transfer the hot butter into a clean, dry metal bowl and refrigerate for 1 hour. Whisk the butter to distribute all of the brown bits evenly throughout. At this point, the butter should be cool enough to transfer to a plastic container. Cover and store in the refrigerator for up to 1 month.

Beurre Monté Yields 2 Cups

INGREDIENTS

1 pound butter, cubed
⅓ cup water

Bring the water to a simmer in a medium-sized pot. Remove the pot from the heat or lower the flame to the lowest setting and whisk in the butter, 1 or 2 cubes at a time, to create an emulsion. Keep the Beurre Monté warm until it's needed, but do not allow it to boil or it will break. This should be made right before it is to be used.

Carrot Stock Yields 2 Cups

Melt the butter in a large, heavy-bottomed pot on medium-high heat. When the butter starts to foam, add the vegetables. Cook until the vegetables start to brown, about 10 minutes. Deglaze the pot with white wine, scraping up all the brown bits left on the bottom of the pot. Add the Chicken Stock and bring to a boil. Lower the heat and simmer for 3 hours. Strain through a chinois and discard the solids. Reduce the liquid in a clean pot until approximately 2 cups remain. Cool immediately and store in the refrigerator.

NOTES
SPECIAL EQUIPMENT: Chinois or fine-mesh strainer.

INGREDIENTS

5 large carrots, thinly sliced
½ cup onion, medium dice
½ cup leeks, medium dice
2 tablespoons butter
1 cup white wine
1 gallon Chicken Stock
   (see page 227)

Chicken Stock Yields 3 Quarts

Thoroughly rinse the bones under cold water to remove any blood and impurities. Combine the bones and water in a large pot. Skim the surface with a ladle as soon as any impurities rise to the surface. Set the flame on high and continue skimming as particles surface.

When the liquid comes to a boil, add the ice and lower the heat to simmer. The ice will cause the fat to coagulate at the surface, making it easier to skim off. Remove as much as possible.

Add the vegetables and herbs, return to a boil, then lower to a simmer. If possible, adjust the stockpot so that just a corner of it is over the heat. This will make it easier to skim. Simmer for 30–40 minutes, skimming occasionally.

Remove the pot from the heat and let the stock rest for 20 minutes to allow any particles to settle on the bottom. Set a chinois over a large container and ladle the liquid through the chinois. Discard the cloudy bottom layer of liquid that may remain in the stockpot, along with the bones. Cool the stock immediately in an ice bath.

NOTES
SPECIAL EQUIPMENT: Chinois or fine-mesh strainer.

NOTE: Chicken Stock can be stored in the refrigerator for up to 5 days or frozen for up to 2 months.

INGREDIENTS

5 pounds chicken bones
1½ cups carrots, large dice
2 cups white onion, large dice
1 cup celery root, large dice
4 quarts cold water
5 cups ice
3 sprigs thyme
3 sprigs parsley

Court Bouillon Yields 1 Gallon

INGREDIENTS

1 fennel bulb, rough chopped
3 stalks celery, rough chopped
1 white onion, rough chopped
½ cup leeks (white and pale green parts only), rough chopped
½ head garlic, rough chopped
1 lemon, sliced
3 sprigs parsley
1 sprig thyme
1 tablespoon black peppercorns
1 tablespoon white peppercorns
1 teaspoon coriander seeds
1 teaspoon fennel seeds
½ cup white wine vinegar
1 gallon water

Combine all ingredients in a large pot and bring it to a boil. Reduce the heat and simmer for 30 minutes. Strain and discard solids. Store in the refrigerator for up to 3 days.

Duck Confit Serves Eight

INGREDIENTS

8 duck legs, skin removed
1–2 quarts duck fat

Confit Spice
1 tablespoon fennel seeds
1 tablespoon green cardamom seeds
1 tablespoon coriander seeds
2 tablespoons salt
2 tablespoons sugar

Add the fennel, cardamom and coriander seeds to a dry sauté pan and lightly toast them over medium heat, stirring or tossing frequently. Remove the spices from the pan and allow to cool. Grind them to a coarse powder.

Combine the ground spices with the salt and sugar. Generously season the duck legs with this confit curing mix. Cover with plastic wrap and refrigerate for 24 hours.

Preheat the oven to 300 degrees. Remove the legs from the refrigerator and thoroughly rinse under cold water. Dry them completely with paper towels and place them in a roasting pan deep enough so they can be covered with the fat.

Bring the duck fat to a boil and pour it over the legs. Cover the pan with foil, transfer it to the oven and cook for 2 hours.

Check for doneness by piercing the leg with a paring knife. If the meat releases easily from the bone, it is done.

Let the legs cool in the pan until the duck fat returns to room temperature. Remove the legs and strain the fat through a chinois so that it can be used for another application. Remove the meat from the bones. The confit can be refrigerated for up to 10 days or frozen until needed.

The confit method is the same for chicken, squab and pheasant. Keep in mind that larger birds will take longer to cook.

NOTES
SPECIAL EQUIPMENT: Electric coffee/spice grinder, chinois or fine-mesh strainer.

Duck Sauce Yields 1 Quart

Preheat the oven to 450 degrees. Place the duck pieces on a sheet tray lined with a rack. Roast for 1 hour or until the pieces have browned. Drain off the excess fat.

Coat the bottom of a large saucepot with grapeseed oil and set on high heat. When the oil is hot, add the onion, carrot and celery root. Sauté until the vegetables are caramelized. Add the tomatoes and the garlic. Cook until the tomatoes break down and start to stick to the pan. Deglaze with the vinegar, scraping up any caramelized bits from the bottom of the pot with a wooden spoon.

Transfer the duck bones to the pot and cover with Chicken Stock. Simmer slowly for 2½–3 hours, skimming the surface periodically. Strain through a chinois. Adjust the seasoning with salt. The sauce can be refrigerated for up to 5 days or frozen for 6 months.

NOTES
SPECIAL EQUIPMENT: Chinois or fine-mesh strainer.

INGREDIENTS

½ cup onion, medium dice
¼ cup carrot, medium dice
¼ cup celery root, peeled and
   medium dice
4 plum tomatoes, quartered
3 cloves garlic, smashed
2 duck carcasses, cut into
   approximately 3-inch pieces
½ cup rice wine vinegar
3 quarts Chicken Stock
   (see page 227)
2 tablespoons grapeseed oil
Salt

Garlic Confit Yields ½ Cup

Combine the garlic and oil in a small, heavy-bottomed saucepot. Place over high heat until the oil begins to get hot, then reduce the flame to its lowest setting. Gently simmer for 1 hour. The garlic should be a golden brown color. Do not allow it to get too dark. Remove the pot from the heat. Let the garlic steep on the stovetop for an additional hour. Transfer to a plastic container and refrigerate for up to a week.

INGREDIENTS

1 head garlic, cloves separated
   and peeled
2 cups extra-virgin olive oil

Mushroom Stock Yields 3 Cups

Wash mushrooms thoroughly in 2 or 3 changes of water. Coarsely chop them and the other vegetables.

Add the mushrooms and vegetables to a large pot and cook on high heat, stirring frequently. The mushrooms will release a lot of water. Cook until nearly all of it evaporates, about 20 minutes. Add the water and bring to a boil. Lower the heat and simmer for 2 hours. Strain through a chinois and cool immediately.

The stock should be dark with an intense mushroom flavor. It can be stored in the refrigerator for up to a week or frozen for 6 months.

NOTES
SPECIAL EQUIPMENT: Chinois or fine-mesh strainer.

INGREDIENTS

2½ pounds white button
   mushrooms
1 large carrot, medium dice
½ onion, medium dice
4 cloves garlic
2 quarts water

Pasta Dough Yields 1 Pound

INGREDIENTS

1 whole egg
6 egg yolks
250 grams (approximately 8.8 ounces) all-purpose flour
Extra bench flour
½ teaspoon olive oil
1 tablespoon milk

Mound the flour on a wooden work surface and create a well in the center. Add the wet ingredients to the well. With two fingers, slowly work the wet ingredients into the flour. When the center is pasty, carefully fold in the remaining flour. Knead the dough for at least 10 minutes or until all the flour has been incorporated and the dough is elastic rather than crumbly. Depending on the relative humidity, you may need more or less flour to achieve this. Remove the dough from the work surface and discard the excess flour. Dust the dough with fresh flour, wrap it in plastic, and allow it to rest for 20–30 minutes. The longer you kneaded it, the longer it needs to rest. The dough is best when used the day it is made.

Roasted Garlic Stock Yields 1 Quart

INGREDIENTS

3–4 heads garlic
2 tablespoons olive oil
½ onion, sliced
2 shallots, sliced
4 basil leaves
4 sprigs thyme
1½ quarts water
Salt and pepper

Preheat the oven to 400 degrees. Cut off the stem ends of the garlic heads to reveal the tops of the cloves. Place on aluminum foil, cut-side up, and drizzle with olive oil. Season with salt and pepper. Tightly close the foil to form a pouch around the garlic. Roast for 40–45 minutes.

Combine the onions, shallots and water in a heavy-bottomed saucepot. Simmer for 15 minutes. Add the head of roasted garlic and mash it into the broth with a whisk. Simmer for an additional 15 minutes. Remove the pot from the stove and add the herbs. Allow the herbs to steep in the stock for 20 minutes. Strain and refrigerate until needed.

NOTES
SPECIAL EQUIPMENT: Chinois or fine-mesh strainer.

Simple Syrup

INGREDIENTS

Equal parts sugar and water

Combine the sugar and water in pot and gently heat until sugar is completely melted, stirring occasionally. Store the syrup in the refrigerator for up to 1 month.

Thyme Oil Yields ¼–⅓ Cup

In a large pot of boiling salted water, blanch the thyme for 35 seconds. Add the parsley and blanch for an additional 15 seconds. Shock the herbs in an ice bath to stop the cooking process. Remove the herbs from the ice and dry as thoroughly as possible.

Transfer the thyme and parsley to a blender. Add 1 or 2 tablespoons of the oil and blend on medium speed just to break up the leaves. Raise the speed to high and add the remaining oil. Puree for 3 minutes. Place the puree in a small bowl sitting in a larger bowl of ice. Stir until the mixture is cold. Transfer to a container and refrigerate for 24 hours.

Line a fine-mesh strainer with a coffee filter and place it over a bowl. Pour the puree into the filter and allow it to strain overnight. Do not try to ring out the filter; this will make the oil cloudy. Pour the oil into a small squeeze bottle and store in the refrigerator.

NOTES
SPECIAL EQUIPMENT: Fine-mesh strainer, coffee filter.

INGREDIENTS

⅓ cup thyme leaves
3 cups flat leaf parsley
¾ cup grapeseed oil

Vegetable Stock Yields 1 Quart

Combine all the ingredients in a large pot and bring it to a boil. Reduce the heat to its lowest setting and simmer for 30 minutes. Strain. Vegetable stock can be refrigerated for up to 5 days.

NOTES
SPECIAL EQUIPMENT: Chinois or fine-mesh strainer.

INGREDIENTS

½ white onion, sliced
1 carrot, rough chopped
3 cloves garlic, smashed
¼ celery root, rough chopped
1 teaspoon fennel seeds
1 teaspoon white peppercorns
4 parsley stems
1½ quarts water

Veal / Lamb Sauce Yields 2 Cups

INGREDIENTS

3 quarts Chicken Stock
  (see page 227)
2 pounds veal bones
Grapeseed oil
1 carrot, large dice
1 cup celery root, large dice
1 white onion, large dice
½ head garlic, halved (skin intact)
4 plum tomatoes, quartered
¼ cup tomato paste
½ cup red wine
4 sprigs thyme
Salt and pepper

This recipe is for veal sauce. For lamb sauce, substitute lamb bones for the veal bones.

Preheat the oven to 450 degrees. Thoroughly rinse the bones and pat dry. Roast the bones on a sheet pan lined with a rack for 45 minutes or until well browned. Remove from the oven and set aside.

Meanwhile, heat a medium stockpot on medium-high heat. Coat the bottom with a thin layer of grapeseed oil. When the oil is hot, add the carrots, celery root, onions and garlic. Season with salt. Cook for 10 minutes, stirring periodically. When the vegetables are browned and nicely caramelized, add the tomatoes and tomato paste. After a few minutes, the tomatoes will begin to break down and stick to the bottom of the pot. Lower the heat to medium and cook for 10–15 minutes, stirring often.

Deglaze the pan with the red wine and scrape up the brown bits stuck to the bottom of the pot with a wooden spoon. Add the Chicken Stock, thyme and bones. Bring to a boil then reduce the flame to the lowest setting and simmer for 1½ hours. Periodically skim the surface of the sauce with a ladle to remove the fat and impurities that have risen to the surface.

Strain the sauce through a chinois and discard the solids. Transfer the sauce to a clean saucepot and return it to the stovetop. Continue to simmer the sauce on the lowest setting until the desired consistency is reached. The sauce is thick enough when it can coat the back of a spoon. Strain the sauce again and adjust the seasoning with salt and pepper.

NOTES
SPECIAL EQUIPMENT: Chinois or fine-mesh strainer.

Specialty Stores

D'ARTAGNAN
Specialty stores nationwide and online
800-DARTAGNAN (327-8246) 973-344-0456
www.Dartagnan.com
Foie gras, duck, wild game, specialty mushrooms, organic
chicken, fresh turkey and other specialty meats.

TSAR NICOULAI CAVIAR
Online retailer
800-95-CAVIAR
www.tsarnicoulai.com
Variety of caviar, caviar accessories, smoked salmon and
smoked sturgeon.

JB PRINCE
36 East 31st Street
New York, NY 10016
800-473-0577
www.jbprince.com
Specialty kitchen gear, immersion thermal circulators,
professional-grade cutlery and professional-grade pots
and pans.

DEAN & DELUCA
Stores in New York, Washington, Napa Valley, Charlotte,
Kansas City
800-221-7714
www.deananddeluca.com
High-end vinegars, oils, olives, cheese and canned goods.

SUR LA TABLE
Stores nationwide
800-243-9852
www.surlatable.com
Professional-grade kitchen equipment, cutlery and cookware.

WILLIAMS-SONOMA
Stores nationwide
800-541-1262
www.williams-sonoma.com
Professional-grade kitchen equipment, cutlery and cookware.

CAMERONS PRODUCTS
Online retailer
888-563-0227
www.cameronscookware.com
Stovetop smokers, stock pots, roasters and other high-quality stainless steel cookware.

FOODSAVER
Online and retail stores nationwide
877-777-8042
www.foodsaver.com
Vacuum sealing systems.

POLYSCIENCE
Online retailer
800-229-7569
www.cuisinetechnology.com
Thermal circulators and vacuum sealers.

CAPFRUIT
Specialty retailers nationwide
+33 (0) 475-31-4022
www.capfruit.com
Fruit purees, coulis and frozen fruit.

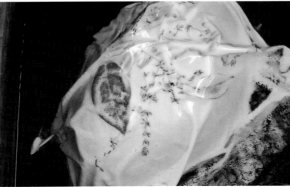

Index